MW01274027

Okanagan Mission Secondary
4544 Gordon Drive
Kelowna, B.C. V1W 1T4

Sexually Transmitted Infections

YOUNG ADULT'S GUIDE TO THE SCIENCE OF HEALTH

Allergies & Asthma

Contraception & Pregnancy

Coping with Moods

Dental Care

Drug- & Alcohol-Related Health Issues

Fitness & Nutrition

Growth & Development

Health Implications of Cosmetic Surgery,
Makeovers, & Body Alterations

Healthy Skin

Managing Stress

Sexually Transmitted Infections

Sleep Deprivation & Its Consequences

Smoking-Related Health Issues

Suicide & Self-Destructive Behaviors

Weight Management

Young Adult's Guide to the Science of Health

Sexually Transmitted Infections

Miranda and William Hunter

MASON CREST

Mason Crest
450 Parkway Drive, Suite D
Broomall, PA 19008
www.masoncrest.com

Printed in the Hashemite Kingdom of Jordan.

First printing
9 8 7 6 5 4 3 2 1

Series ISBN: 978-1-4222-2803-6
Hardcover ISBN: 978-1-4222-2814-2
Paperback ISBN: 978-1-4222-3007-7
ebook ISBN: 978-1-4222-9010-1

The Library of Congress has cataloged the
    hardcopy format(s) as follows:

        Library of Congress Cataloging-in-Publication Data

Hunter, Miranda, 1977-
  Sexually transmitted infections / Miranda Hunter, William Hunter.
      pages cm. – (Young adult's guide to the science of health)
  Includes index.
  ISBN 978-1-4222-2814-2 (hardcover) – ISBN 978-1-4222-2803-6 (series) – ISBN 978-1-4222-9010-1
(ebook) – ISBN 978-1-4222-3007-7 (paperback)
  1. Sexual health–Juvenile literature. 2. Sexually transmitted diseases–Juvenile literature.
  3. Teenagers–Sexual behavior–Juvenile literature. I. Hunter, William, 1971- II. Title.
  RA788.H86 2014
  614.5'470835–dc23
                    2013006390

Designed and produced by Vestal Creative Services.
www.vestalcreative.com

This book is meant to educate and should not be used as an alternative
to appropriate medical care. Its creators have made every effort to en-
sure that the information presented is accurate and up to date—but this
book is not intended to substitute for the help and services of trained
medical professionals.

Contents

Introduction

by Dr. Sara Forman

You're not a little kid anymore. When you look in the mirror, you probably see a new person, someone who's taller, bigger, with a face that's starting to look more like an adult's than a child's. And the changes you're experiencing on the inside may be even more intense than the ones you see in the mirror. Your emotions are changing, your attitudes are changing, and even the way you think is changing. Your friends are probably more important to you than they used to be, and you no longer expect your parents to make all your decisions for you. You may be asking more questions and posing more challenges to the adults in your life. You might experiment with new identities—new ways of dressing, hairstyles, ways of talking—as you try to determine just who you really are. Your body is maturing sexually, giving you a whole new set of confusing and exciting feelings. Sorting out what is right and wrong for you may seem overwhelming.

Growth and development during adolescence is a multifaceted process involving every aspect of your being. It all happens so fast that it can be confusing and distressing. But this stage of your life is entirely normal. Every adult in your life made it through adolescence—and you will too.

But what exactly is adolescence? According to the American Heritage Dictionary, adolescence is "the period of physical and psychological development from the onset of puberty to adulthood." What does this really mean?

In essence, adolescence is the time in our lives when the needs of childhood give way to the responsibilities of adulthood. According to psychologist Erik Erikson, these years are a time of separation and individuation. In other words, you are separating from your parents, becoming an individual in your own right. These are the years when you begin to make decisions on your own. You are becoming more self-reliant and less dependent on family members.

When medical professionals look at what's happening physically—what they refer to as the biological model—they define the teen years as a period of hormonal transformation toward sexual maturity, as well as a time of peak growth, second only to the growth during the months of infancy. This physical transformation from childhood to adulthood takes place under the influence of society's norms and social pressures; at the same time your body is changing, the people around you are expecting new things from you. This is what makes adolescence such a unique and challenging time.

Being a teenager in North America today is exciting yet stressful. For those who work with teens, whether by parenting them, educating them, or providing services to them, adolescence can be challenging as well. Youth are struggling with many messages from society and the media about how they should behave and who they should be. "Am I normal?" and "How do I fit in?" are often questions with which teens wrestle. They are facing decisions about their health such as how to take care of their bodies, whether to use drugs and alcohol, or whether to have sex.

This series of books on adolescents' health issues provides teens, their parents, their teachers, and all those who work with them accurate information and the tools to keep them safe and healthy. The topics include information about:

- normal growth
- social pressures
- emotional issues
- specific diseases to which adolescents are prone
- stressors facing youth today
- sexuality

The series is a dynamic set of books, which can be shared by youth and the adults who care for them. By providing this information to educate in these areas, these books will help build a foundation for readers so they can begin to work on improving the health and well-being of youth today.

1

Baby-Making Body Parts and the Bugs That Bug Them

Mike was a handsome young man. His girlfriends were always the envy of the other girls at school. He was smart, athletic, and fun. He loved to party. Mike almost never missed school. In fact, he only missed four days in three years of high school. He played sports in every season and did not like to miss practices or games. The teachers all thought of Mike as a model citizen, the perfect student. He surely had a bright future.

Mike never stayed with one girlfriend for very long. There were so many girls that wanted to date him that he had no trouble finding a new girl very quickly after breaking up with one. Mike's girlfriends were so honored by his attention that even "nice girls" had sex with him. He even dated girls from other schools.

One day, the phone rang. It was a doctor from the health department, explaining that one of Mike's ex-girlfriends had a serious infection called syphilis. They had gotten Mike's name from her because it was standard practice to call all a patient's sexual partners following diagnosis of syphilis. They wanted Mike to come in and get tested as soon as possible. He was shocked and scared. He had heard of syphilis and knew it was a sexually transmitted infection. What would happen to his reputation if people found out about this? The doctor assured Mike that they would not tell anyone. Mike made an appointment to get tested.

Mike went to the health department clinic the following Saturday. He was very nervous. The nurses asked him to put on an exam gown and sit in a quiet room until the doctor could see him. The doctor came in and asked Mike if he could take a few samples. He told Mike he would call when the samples had been examined.

When the phone rang two days later, Mike ran to answer. The doctor was on the other line. He told Mike he had syphilis and wanted a list of all of Mike's sexual partners. Mike gave the names, and the doctor told him to go to the local pharmacy. He had to pick up a prescription for some drugs that would, hopefully, clear up the infection before it did lasting damage. Mike was stunned. How could he be infected? He showered every day, ate right, and only slept with the most attractive girls.

Mike was one of the causes of a large syphilis outbreak at his school. Many of his sexual partners were infected and had to be treated. Some of them had had sex with other boys, spreading the infection further. The doctors at the health department had their hands full trying to contain the outbreak, but in the end, they were successful. Mike had unknowingly been an infected host of a potentially deadly infection for many months. He was lucky the infection was discovered.

Sexually Transmitted Infections

Engaging in risky behaviors is like shooting an arrow at your own head!

The human body has been called a playground for diseases. Tiny, microscopic organisms cause most of these illnesses and are specially adapted to live in our bodies. These organisms, sometimes called "microbes," "germs," or "bugs," can be bacteria, protists, fungi, or viruses. The symptoms that we feel when we get sick are side effects of the daily life functions of these tiny creatures. When microbes that are not normally there invade our bodies, we call it an infection. If those microbes make us sick, we call it a disease. It is important to remember, though, that our bodies are always full of bacteria and fungi that are actually good for us in some ways. Normally, the bacteria and fungi in our bodies are kept under control by our immune system, which is there to respond to and fight against infection.

Not all infections cause disease. Sometimes, the organisms will infect a person without causing any symptoms. An infection that has no symptoms can still be passed from person to person. These are often the most difficult types of infection to prevent and cure, because we often do not even know we are infected.

The various types of microbes affect us in different ways. Bacterial, protist, and fungal infections affect our bodies because their waste products can leave us feeling ill, weakened, or worse. Viral infections, on the other hand, affect our cells, causing them to not function properly. Some viruses actually attack the cells that make up our immune system, weakening or blocking our ability to fight off infections.

Bacteria

Bacteria are a common cause of disease in people. They are single-celled organisms that are usually found on just about everything in the world. Thankfully, most types of bacteria do not cause disease under normal circumstances. Most bacteria

Sexually Transmitted Infections

MYTHS AND MISCONCEPTIONS

TEST YOUR STI IQ.

Even though Sexually Transmitted Infections are relatively common, there are many myths and misconceptions that have circulated for many years. As you read through this book, look for the truth about these points. For a complete explanation, turn to page 119.

MYTHS:

1. Only people who have sex with many different partners get STIs.
2. I can't get an STI because I am taking birth control pills.
3. Douching after sex will protect me from an STI.
4. Using two condoms is even safer than using just one.
5. Having anal sex protects against STIs.
6. Anybody that has had an STI and been successfully treated for it is immune to getting it again.
7. If I don't have any symptoms, I can't have an STI.
8. If I always use a condom, I can't get an STI.
9. Oral sex is safe without a condom.
10. You can't get an STI the first time you have sex.

Most of the time, infections are discovered through some form of medical detective work. The United States Centers for Disease Control (CDC) in Atlanta, Georgia, and the Canadian Centre for **INFECTIOUS** Disease Prevention and Control (CIDPC), in Ottawa, Ontario, are two organizations that track the spread of communicable diseases. Sometimes they are forced to track the spread of STIs by finding the sexual partners of someone known to be infected and following the trail as far as they can. The investigators basically connect the dots until they find the source.

are small enough that it takes millions of them to cover the head of a pin. The fact that they are small is no reason to take them lightly, though. What makes them dangerous is the rate at which they reproduce. Some types of bacteria can double their numbers in less than twenty minutes. One single bacterium does not make us feel ill, but at that rate, one bacterium becomes one million in just under seven hours. We tend to notice that!

Bacterial infections can be treated with antibiotics, a category of drugs used to cure infections caused by bacteria. There are many types of antibiotics in use today in North America. Unfortunately, antibiotics are no use against infections caused by viruses, protists, or fungi. Even though the vulnerability of bacteria to antibiotics is an advantage, they can be very difficult to get rid of because bacteria quickly develop antibiotic resistance, forcing us to find newer and stronger antibiotics.

Protists

Protists are less common than bacteria, but no less important. They are typically larger and more complex than bacteria and far more mobile. While most protists do not affect people at all, some are parasites. This means they live inside other organisms, including humans. They take what they need to survive and reproduce from their host, which is what we call the body that they live in and feed off. They affect people in much the same way that bacteria do. When the protist population grows to a large enough size, the waste products they produce begin to make us feel ill. Protists are easily passed back and forth when their human hosts are in close contact with each other. In the United States and Canada, there are few drugs approved for treatment of protist infections.

Fungi

Fungi are single-celled organisms that grow in colonies. They do not usually cause problems in people, but when the conditions are right, fungi can grow quickly and cause disease. Fungi known as yeasts cause most of the fungal diseases in humans. Most often, yeasts live in a balance with other microbes in the body. However, when the balance is changed, the yeasts can take over and cause health problems. This sometimes happens when a person takes an antibiotic to fight off a bacterial infection. The antibiotics also kill the good bacteria in the body that usually keep the fungi in check, but have no effect on the fungi. This causes the balance to be shifted in favor of the yeast, allowing them to grow rapidly. Luckily, antifungal medicines can prevent or stop fungal infections.

Viruses

Viruses are among the most common causes of disease in the world. They are the smallest of all the microbes. In fact, some viruses are actually small enough to infect bacteria! Their small size makes them particularly easy to spread. Some types can actually float long distances through the air. Many people do not consider viruses alive, because they do not have any function at all until they get inside a host. Once inside, they attach themselves to the host's cells and begin to produce many copies of themselves inside the cells. Usually the process of copying causes the host cell to die, making the host sick. They take over and use the cells of our bodies, bursting the cell membranes and killing the cells. Viruses are far less treatable than the other disease-causing microbes because they do not respond to many

medicines. Antibiotics have no effect on them at all. There are very few antiviral medicines that are in use today.

Sexually Transmitted Infections

Some of the most common types of diseases are sexually transmitted infections (STIs), meaning that they are passed by sexual contact. STIs have been a problem for people since the beginning of recorded time. Gonorrhea got its name in Greece in the second century and was a major problem in ancient Egypt and China. Syphilis, a particularly deadly STI when it is left untreated, was one of the major causes of death in Europe for centuries. It may even have affected the ancient native civilizations of Central and South America as well. Although these infections were not well understood, they killed millions of people throughout the centuries.

The Human Body

The human body contains many internal parts that are known as organs. Each one has a special function, and examples are the brain, stomach, heart, and lungs. These organs can be grouped into eleven major organ systems. For example, when we eat, we use our digestive system. When we breathe, we use our respiratory system. Most of these organ systems have a particular function that helps us get through each and every day. There is one system that is not required for everyday life: the reproductive system. This system's only function is sexual reproduction, making babies.

The Reproductive System

Sometimes, we call them our "privates." Little kids call them their "pee-pees," "woo-woos," or sometimes just "down there." They are, for some people, a source of embarrassment, and they just can't quite bring themselves to use the technical names. We are talking, of course, about the outer parts of the reproductive system. It is important to understand our bodies and how they work in order to help us protect them. Throughout this book we will talk about STIs and the effect they have on these parts and the rest of our bodies.

Some people find it difficult to talk about the reproductive system because it is usually thought of as private or personal. It is a fairly delicate system, and our hesitation to talk about some parts of this system is one of the reasons that it is so commonly affected by infections, especially STIs. It is common for people to avoid getting proper medical care, even if they are obviously infected. Many STIs have very easily identified signs, such as pain while urinating, **DISCHARGE**, blisters, or swelling. Ignoring these signs can be very dangerous.

There are many differences between the reproductive systems of men and women. In general, the organs are similar between men and women, but their functions are very different. Both have a system of tubes and glands that are necessary for

The term "sexually transmitted diseases" (also called STDs) has fallen out of favor with some scientists. They now prefer "STI," which stands for sexually transmitted infection, rather than disease. This term is more accurate, because many STIs do not have any symptoms, making them infections and not diseases.

In the past, STIs were known as venereal diseases (VD) and are still sometimes called VDs. The name "venereal" comes from Venus, the ancient Roman goddess of love.

Sexually Transmitted Infections

reproduction. Each system has secondary sex organs, which are outside the body and primary sex organs that are inside the body. Throughout this book we will use the term genitals to refer to the external sexual organs.

The Male Reproductive System

Much of the reproductive system of males is outside the body. Its entire function is to deliver sperm to fertilize an egg, which will ultimately grow into a baby. The penis is the most obvious sexual organ and has multiple functions. It is also a part of the urinary system, since urine passes through the penis. The penis is made up of a shaft of **ERECTILE TISSUE**, through which many blood vessels pass, and the glans, or head, which has a high concentration of nerves. The blood vessels in the penis allow a man's penis to become erect, or hard. An erection occurs for various reasons, including sexual arousal. In order for an erection to occur, the erectile tissue becomes flooded with blood. Erections are a very important part of sexual reproduction, though not absolutely necessary to produce a baby.

Sperm are produced and stored in a series of tiny muscular tubes called the epididymis, found on the back of the testicles. The epididymis is connected to the vas deferens, the tube that connects the testicles to the urethra, the tube that carries sperm and urine out of the body. When a man is about to ejaculate, or orgasm, contractions of the epididymis force the sperm out of the vas deferens and into the urethra.

The fluid that a man ejaculates, called semen, is actually made up of sperm and a couple different fluids. One of these fluids is produced by the **PROSTATE** gland and lubricates the sperm and allows them to swim. Another fluid is made in the seminal vesicle, a small gland found near the prostate. This fluid feeds

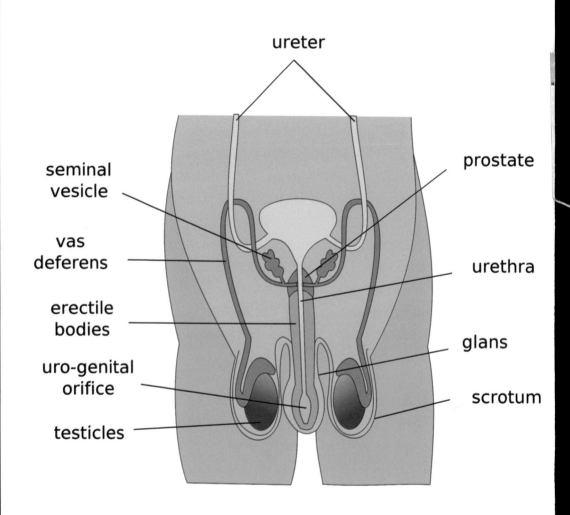

Male reproductive system.

Sexually Transmitted Infections

the sperm while they swim in order to keep them alive long enough to do their job. One of the main functions of semen is to neutralize the acid in a woman's vagina, allowing the sperm to survive long enough to fertilize an egg.

Sperm are relatively delicate. Without the other fluids in semen, sperm would probably be killed by the acid in a woman's vagina and would not be able to fertilize an egg. They also must be stored at a lower temperature than the normal body temperature of 98.6°F (37°C). In order to keep them cool, the testicles are contained in a pocket of skin outside the body, called the **SCROTUM**. It can actually respond to external temperatures by tightening up or relaxing. When the temperature outside the body is high, the scrotum relaxes. When the temperature is low, the scrotum tightens up, drawing the testicles up into the body to keep them warm.

Female Reproductive System

The female reproductive system is almost all inside the body. In fact, the only parts that can be seen by looking at the outside of the body are the breasts, labia, and clitoris. Although breasts have no part in creating a child, they are quite important for raising a child, so they are considered part of the reproductive system. The female reproductive system is more complex than the male reproductive system, because it has more functions. While the male system only needs to deliver sperm, the female system must produce the eggs, protect and nourish the developing fetus, give birth, and feed the infant after birth.

The female genitals consist of the breasts, labia, and clitoris. The breasts are mostly fatty tissue, but also contain the mammary glands, which produce milk to feed an infant. The labia are folds of skin that cover and protect the opening of the vagina, the entrance to the inside part of the female reproductive system. There are actually two sets of labia; the labia majora are on the outside, and underneath are the labia minora. The clitoris is a small bud of skin and nerves attached to the upper portion of the labia minora. Its function is mainly for sexual stimulation. In the same region, the female urethra empties the bladder just above the vaginal opening under the labia minora.

The vagina is also known as the birth canal. It is a short, muscular tube that is about eight to ten centimeters long. The vagina is lined with mucous membranes that produce fluid to lubricate it. The mucus is relatively acidic, which helps prevent infection by bacteria and fungi. Women who have not had sex may have a hymen, a thin membrane that stretches across the opening of the vagina. Sometimes a woman will experience bleeding and pain during her first sexual intercourse because the hymen is ruptured by the man's penis. It is also common for a young woman to rupture her hymen accidentally while inserting tampons, during medical examinations, or during exercise.

The vagina connects to the uterus inside the body. The uterus is where an egg normally develops into an infant after being successfully fertilized. The opening of the uterus is called the cervix. Like the vagina, the uterus is a muscular tube lined with mucous membranes. The eggs descend from the OVA-RIES and implant in the walls of the uterus each month. The monthly menstruation, or period, is the shedding of the uterine lining and unfertilized egg.

At the top of the uterus, there are two tubes that connect to the ovaries. These tubes are called fallopian tubes. These are about ten centimeters long and lined with tiny hair-like fibers called cilia. These move in a wave-like fashion to push the egg from the ovary into the uterus. Sometimes the eggs implant in the fallopian tubes and are fertilized there instead of the uterus. This is a condition known as an ectopic pregnancy, which can be deadly.

Sexually Transmitted Infections

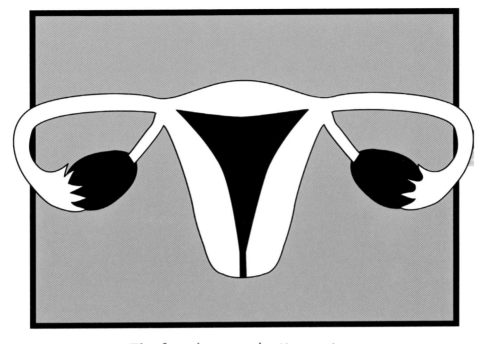

The female reproductive system.

The ovaries produce the eggs, which will develop into a baby when combined with a sperm. They also function as glands that release hormones. The ovaries are almond shaped and about three centimeters long, one centimeter wide, and one centimeter thick. They release one egg about every twenty-eight days in response to the normal menstrual cycle.

Vulnerability to Infections

Because the reproductive system is considered private, many people will not openly discuss issues related to it. Doctors cannot diagnose potential problems without being told of symptoms and being given an opportunity to examine a patient. In addition, many of the medicines used to cure these infections cannot be prescribed without a doctor's permission.

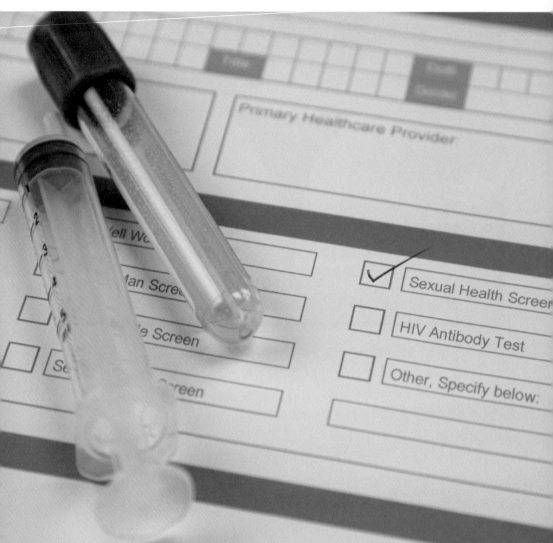

Blood tests can determine if you have certain STIs.

The tissues of many parts of the reproductive system are not easily visible. Special tools must be used to examine them for signs of infection. A skin rash may be a sign that we need to see a doctor, but such symptoms are less easy to see with many parts of the reproductive system. Usually, infections begin with

Sexually Transmitted Infections

mild symptoms and get progressively worse until they are cured. Some STIs do not display symptoms until several weeks or even years have passed since the time of infection. This does not mean they are not doing damage or being passed to unprotected sexual partners! Human immunodeficiency virus (HIV) is one example of this type of infection. HIV is a deadly virus that cannot be cured but is easily passed from partner to partner. Its symptoms often are not seen until nearly ten years have passed (we will discuss HIV more in chapter 6)!

The human reproductive system is one of the most **VULNERABLE** organ systems of the human body. Since most of the organs are found near exits from the body, it is relatively easy for disease-causing microbes to get into it. Most other organs are found deep within the body, wrapped in special tissues that protect them from harm. This is not the case with the reproductive system. It is one of the only places in our bodies that microbes can enter and exit with ease. The surfaces of the reproductive system are all lined with moist warm tissues where microbes love to live.

These microbes are like destructive gang members that move in on otherwise healthy and peaceful territory. The chapters that follow will describe the cast of characters that make up the STI gang.

2

Gonorrhea:
The Dreaded Drip

Kyle was Abby's first real boyfriend. She had gone out on dates with several guys, but she didn't get serious with anyone. When Kyle asked her to the Homecoming Dance, she was excited and nervous. Kyle was so cute! He turned out to be a really nice guy, and they had a wonderful time at the dance. Before she knew it, people were referring to them as a couple, and she was spending all her spare time with him.

After she had been dating Kyle for several months, things started to get more intense between them. Abby was a virgin, but Kyle wasn't.

Although Abby's parents had always told her to wait until she was married to have sex, she thought it was okay as long as they were in love. The first few times they were together, they used condoms; they knew they weren't ready for a baby. After a while, Kyle suggested that Abby go on the birth control pill. She felt embarrassed talking about that type of thing with him, so she quickly agreed, even though she would have preferred to continue using condoms.

A few weeks later, Abby went to her doctor for a physical so she could join the track team. She mentioned to the doctor that she had been having some spotting in between her periods and some discomfort when she went to the bathroom. The doctor did a pelvic exam and told her he would call her in a few days. After a couple days, the

Sexually Transmitted Infections

doctor's office asked her to come back in for another appointment. The doctor told her he had some serious news. Abby had gonorrhea.

She was so embarrassed! Even though she could take some medicine that would clear up the infection, she was afraid that someone would find out. How could she fill the prescription without her parents knowing? Plus, the doctor said that the only way she could have gotten it was from having sex with someone who had gonorrhea. That meant Kyle had it too! Had he been cheating on her or had he had it for months? How was she ever going to get the courage to talk to him? This was so much worse than it would have been to talk to him about condoms in the first place!

Gonorrhea, also known as "the Clap" or "the Drip," is one of the oldest known sexually transmitted infections; it was given its name almost two thousand years ago. It is very common in North America, with 321,849 new cases reported in the United States during 2011, according to the United States Centers for Disease Control (CDC). The rate of infection in the United States is about 105 people for each 100,000. Of course, these are only the reported cases. Officials estimate that about twice that number are actually infected each year.

The good news is that gonorrhea can be cured completely with antibiotics, but only people who seek medical treatment will be cured. Those that do not see a doctor will continue to

Gonorrhea got its name in the year 131 CE from one of the greatest Greek physicians, Galen. The name literally means "flow of seed." Galen chose this name because he mistakenly believed that the discharge from a man's penis was seeds flowing out against his will.

Gonorrhea rates have started to slowly increase in the United States. However, rates are on the rise among teenagers. Around 62 percent of reported cases of gonorrhea are found in people between the ages of fifteen and twenty-four. The infection is especially common among African Americans, who account for two-thirds of all reported gonorrhea cases.

spread the infection to others and can have serious medical problems themselves.

Cause and Transmission of Gonorrhea

Gonorrhea is caused by a bacterium, Neisseria gonorrhoeae, which grows and flourishes in the warm, moist areas of the body, such as the cervix and uterus in women and the urethra, throat, anus or even eyes in women and men. It typically spreads from person to person through sexual contact, and is passed very easily during sex, whether it is vaginal, anal, or oral. The bacteria are in the semen, discharge, or vaginal fluids of an infected person. They most often infect the urethra in men and the cervix in women.

Women are more likely to get the infection than men. This may be because the semen with the bacteria in it stays in the woman's vagina after sex, allowing more time for the infection to spread. Men tend to remain in contact with the vaginal fluids of their female partners only during intercourse. A woman who has unprotected sex with an infected man has a 50 percent chance of getting the infection, while a man who has unprotected sex with a woman with gonorrhea has only a 30 percent chance of being infected.

Most of the "bugs" that cause STIs cannot be seen without the help of a microscope.

GONORRHEA: The Dreaded Drip

True love may be romantic—but it can also be risky.

Sexually Transmitted Infections

Gonorrhea can also spread to other areas of the body. For example, if Abby had come into contact with the bacteria by touching an infected area of Kyle's body, she could have gotten an infection in her eyes if she touched them without washing her hands first. Once a person is already infected, she can spread it to other parts of her own body that are warm and moist. This sort of transmission must happen quite quickly, because the bacteria cannot survive outside of a warm, moist area for very long. As a result, gonorrhea is highly unlikely to be passed by sharing towels or sitting on a toilet seat.

The infection can also be passed from an infected woman to her baby during childbirth. Most women today are tested for gonorrhea during pregnancy. Almost all babies are treated soon after birth with eye drops that kill gonorrhea bacteria, just in case their mother has the infection and does not know it. An untreated eye infection would very likely lead to blindness in the child.

Symptoms and Complications of Gonorrhea

Many people have no symptoms at all when they become infected with gonorrhea. A quarter to a half of all women and about ten percent of men infected do not have any symptoms at all. Kyle, the young man in our story, may not have known he was infected. However, he may also have had symptoms that he was too embarrassed to talk about. Most people who have symptoms of gonorrhea have them within several days after the sexual encounter. However, the symptoms could start as soon as the next day or might not develop for several weeks.

Some symptoms of gonorrhea are similar for men and women. Most people who have gonorrhea will have discharge or fluid coming from their genitals. Usually, there will be a large amount of yellow or greenish discharge, but sometimes people will have small amounts of clear discharge. Both men and women may have pain when they urinate. An untreated infection of the urethra could cause scarring, which could lead to long-term problems with urination.

Anal, throat, or eye infections can occur in people regardless of gender. Anal infections often have no symptoms but can result in pain, discharge, itching, or bleeding. Throat infections also tend to be without symptoms, though a person might have a sore throat. These infections happen most often from sexual encounters during which a male puts his penis into the anus or throat of his sexual partner. Eye infections can be very unpleasant, with redness, thick yellow discharge, and problems seeing. If not treated promptly, blindness can result as well.

Other symptoms depend largely upon the gender of the infected person. A man's infection might move into his prostate, which can cause pain between his testicles and anus, the need to urinate often, and problems urinating. It could also move into the tube that carries sperm from his testicles. This could cause swelling and scarring that could make it difficult for a man to father a child.

Gonorrhea PID (explained on page 38) carries great risk of infertility for women with the infection. The first time a woman has PID, she already has a 10 to 15 percent chance of losing her ability to have a baby. If she gets it again, she has a 25 percent chance of becoming infertile.

Sexually Transmitted Infections

Learning to take care of yourself is an important part of becoming an adult.

Women with cervical infections will often have spotting, or light bleeding, in between periods or after having sex. Pregnant women with gonorrhea are more likely to have problems during the pregnancy, including miscarriage or early delivery. In 10 to 20 percent of women with gonorrhea, their infection will move from the cervix into the uterus, fallopian tubes, and ovaries. This is called pelvic inflammatory disease (PID), a serious condition that can be caused by various STIs. If a woman has PID, she may have pain in her pelvis, pain during sex, and fever in addition to the other symptoms of gonorrhea. As the woman's body tries to fight the infection, her fallopian tubes, which are only about as big as a hair, can swell and fill with pus. If treated promptly, the swelling and blockage might go away, but it might cause scarring that will permanently affect the woman's ability to have a baby. Her eggs may not be able to get out of her fallopian tubes, which could keep her from getting pregnant. It could also result in an ectopic or tubal pregnancy, where the fertilized egg develops in the fallopian tube instead of the uterus. In this case, if the pregnancy is not ended, the baby will soon become too large for the fallopian tube and it will burst, causing her to bleed internally. Without surgery, the woman will die.

Although it is quite rare, untreated gonorrhea infections can travel through a person's blood to other parts of the body. Between 0.5 and 3 percent of people with gonorrhea develop this condition, which is called disseminated gonococcal infection (DGI), or gonococcal arthritis. DGI can result in painful bumps or pimples on the skin, swelling and pain around the liver, or pain and swelling in joints, such as knees or hips. Very rarely, the DGI can get into a person's heart, brain, or spinal cord and cause serious problems, even death.

Abby, the girl in our story, probably had cervical gonorrhea, which may also have spread to her urethra. She did not have many symptoms, but she did have some spotting and pain during urination. Luckily, she told her doctor about these problems before the infection spread to other parts of her body. With treatment, she will probably make a full recovery.

Testing and Treatment for Gonorrhea

If a doctor suspects a person may have gonorrhea, she will take swabs from any area that may have come into contact with the bacteria. A doctor can do several things to diagnose the infection. For instance, she can look at a discharge sample under a microscope, which might give some information about the problem. In addition, the doctor can do tests that day that will give some information about the bacteria. The doctor can rule out gonorrhea with these tests, but she cannot tell for sure if it is gonorrhea. Other tests will take more time and may require that samples be sent out to a laboratory for further testing.

Obviously, gonorrhea can have lasting effects if not treated promptly. With early treatment and modern antibiotics, almost all gonorrhea infections can be completely cured. Unfortunately, some people still believe that infections can be treated by flushing out the penis or vagina of the infected person with various solutions. This is uncomfortable and ineffective. The only way to cure gonorrhea and avoid its dangerous consequences is to take an antibiotic.

During World War II, penicillin was given to injured soldiers to prevent infections. The field medics eventually realized that penicillin also cured some of the STIs the men already had, including gonorrhea. For many years, penicillin was the standard treatment for the infection. A single massive injection of penicillin would typically cure nearly 100 percent of the cases in one night. However, gonorrhea bacteria are very adaptable and have become quite resistant to penicillin over the years.

Today, doctors have several types of antibiotics that are used to treat gonorrhea. As resistant strains continue to develop, doctors continue to change the antibiotics used. If a patient does not respond to the first one prescribed, the doctor will try another. These medications include cephalosporin, which can be given as a single dose by mouth or as a single injection, and various quinolone drugs, all taken in a single oral dose. If gonorrhea is more advanced, more intensive antibiotic treatment could be necessary. Patients should be sure to follow all of their doctor's directions and take all of a medication even if the symptoms stop, because failure to do so can contribute to the growing problem of **ANTIBIOTIC-RESISTANT** bacteria. People with gonorrhea are often also treated for chlamydia, unless it has been ruled out by testing, because 50 percent of people with gonorrhea also have chlamydia (see chapter 4).

Abby's doctor would probably have given her the medicine mentioned above, either an injection or some pills to take. Since she was treated relatively soon after infection, she would likely have recovered quite quickly and completely. She would, however, have needed to make sure that Kyle was cured before they had sexual contact again. Otherwise, she would have risked reinfection. Abby was very lucky that she talked with her doctor about the problems she was having so that she avoided the more serious physical consequences. Of course, she still had to deal with the personal and emotional consequences of her actions.

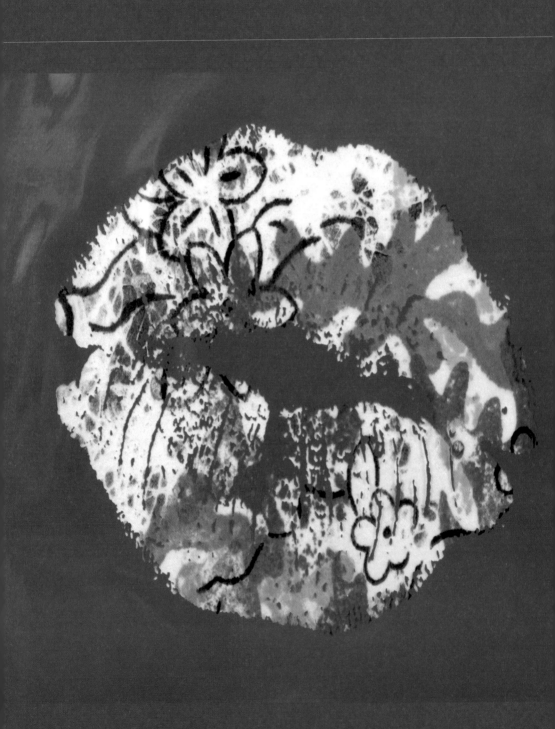

3

Syphilis:
The Impersonator

Kristin was so excited! Her parents finally agreed to let her go away for spring break with her best friend's family. Hanging out with Sarah was the greatest because her parents pretty much let them do whatever they wanted. When they arrived at the hotel, Kristin and Sarah threw on their cutest bathing suits and rushed out to the beach. The girls soaked up some sun and headed in for a quick dinner with Sarah's parents. After eating, the girls went back down to the beach to scope things out. There

Alcohol abuse can increase your vulnerability to various dangers.

Sexually Transmitted Infections

were fires and groups of kids clustered together, listening to music and laughing. Kristin and Sarah didn't want to look too eager, but they were thrilled when some of the guys in one of the nearest groups called out to them as they went past. Kristin was nervous as they walked over. These kids were at least two or three years older than she was, and the guys were much cuter than the boys back home. Kristin soon found herself in the midst of the laughing group, smiling and flirting. Before she knew it, someone had put a beer in her hand. Kristin didn't normally drink, but she didn't want these kids to think she was immature, so she drank it. Several drinks later, Kristin hardly knew where she was. The rest of the night was a blur.

When Kristin woke up the next morning, her head was spinning and her stomach felt sick. She felt sore and sticky between her legs, and she didn't even know how she had gotten home. Kristin stayed close to the hotel for the rest of the vacation. Although Sarah continued to hang out with the kids they'd met the first night, Kristin begged off, making excuses to stay at the hotel. She got her period before they left, so at least she wasn't pregnant.

When Kristin got home, she decided to try to put the whole thing behind her. A funny sore between her legs kept reminding her, but it didn't hurt, and she decided just to ignore it. She really didn't want to admit to anyone, even Sarah, what had happened. After a couple weeks, the sore went away.

Several months later, Kristin came down with a flu bug of some sort. When she broke out in a rash a couple days later, her mother put some cream on the bumps and insisted she go the doctor's office. The doctor asked her questions, many of which were quite embarrassing. She told Kristin that she might have an STI. Kristin had to stay home until the results of a blood test came back so she didn't get anyone else sick with her rash. Kristin didn't know what to tell her mother, but she made an excuse and waited by the phone to hear from the doctor.

Syphilis: The Impersonator

When the phone rang two days later, Kristin answered the phone with a trembling hand. The voice on the other end was kind, but it told her what she hadn't wanted to hear: Kristin had syphilis. The doctor wanted to know the names of all of Kristin's sexual partners; Kristin was embarrassed to confess she didn't know the names. The doctor even insisted that Kristin tell her mother, because her mother could have been infected when she put the cream on Kristin's rash. Kristin hung up the phone with a sick feeling in the pit of her stomach.

Syphilis is one of the only STIs with a history longer than gonorrhea. Some **ARCHAEOLOGISTS** believe that people have suffered from syphilis at least as far back as the ancient civilizations of Central and South America. The infection was first noted in Europe in the late fifteenth century, around the time of Christopher Columbus's return from his travels. Some people speculate that his crew brought it back from either the Americas or West Africa.

The infection may not have been too terrible when it first arrived on the European continent. However, at some point the bacteria **EVOLVED** into a horrible killer. Approximately 10 million people died in a syphilis **EPIDEMIC** in the late fifteenth and early sixteenth centuries, during its first outbreak. The infection caused extremely high fevers and open sores, killing nearly everyone infected with it, some within days. If it arrived with the explorers, as historians suspect, it cannot have been as fast acting or deadly as it was during this later outbreak. Otherwise, the explorers would not have lived to carry the infection to Europe.

The extremely deadly strain that killed so many may have died out during that period. The syphilis bacteria that has made people ill in the hundreds of years since the epidemic and that continues to make people sick today is not nearly so fast-acting.

46

Sexually Transmitted Infections

Syphilis has struck some famous individuals throughout history. The infection made its way from Europe to Asia in the body of the explorer, Vasco de Gama, and likely came to North America with other explorers. Al Capone, one of the most famous American gangsters, suffered from syphilis. In fact, in spite of treatment by prison doctors at Alcatraz, Capone's syphilis progressed to the point that some say he had completely lost his mind by the time of his death in 1947.

Although it can ultimately cause death, it takes many years to do so. It is now often called the "great imitator," because so many of its symptoms are like other infections. As a result, people are often misdiagnosed and do not receive appropriate treatment early on, a problem that sometimes results in lasting damage.

The United States Public Health Service and the Tuskegee Institute conducted a nearly forty-year study of the effects of untreated syphilis starting in 1932. The subjects of this study, 399 poor African American men with LATENT syphilis in Alabama, went completely untreated for the entire forty years. The most educated of these men had finished seventh grade. Government doctors told them they had a condition called "bad blood," and the men were never told they were part of a study. Even though the infection could have been completely cured with penicillin midway through the study, the doctors never offered the medicine or even told the men they had syphilis. By the time the study was stopped, after the public discovered the study was taking place, many of the men had died from the thirty-eight years without treatment. At least twenty-eight and maybe as many as a hundred died from the effects of the infection. In response to the horrified public, the government paid about $10 million dollars to the men in an out-of-court settlement, less than $40,000 a piece.

Cause and Transmission of Syphilis

Syphilis is caused by the bacteria *Treponema pallidum*. These bacteria have an interesting corkscrew shape and thrive in the same warm, moist areas of the human body that the gonorrhea bacteria love. Syphilis is usually passed from person to person through intimate sexual contact. The bacteria are carried in the blood, semen, and vaginal fluids of an infected person. However, when the infection progresses further, it can be spread without sexual contact, through the sores that open up on nonsexual areas of the body. The rash that the girl in our story had was contagious and could have passed to her mother or anyone else who came into contact with it. The bacteria could have entered Kristin's mother's body through tiny breaks in her skin, so small they could not have been seen with the naked eye. They could have also gotten on her hands when she spread the cream on Kristin's rash. If she touched a mucous membrane, such as the inside of her mouth or nose, without washing her hands, the bacteria could have entered through those more vulnerable areas.

Syphilis bacteria, like those that cause gonorrhea, cannot survive outside the warm, moist areas of the body. Therefore, it cannot be passed on towels or toilet seats, contrary to popular myth.

Symptoms and Complications of Syphilis

Once people are infected with syphilis, they will go through four steps of illness unless they are treated for the infection. Dur-

Soap and water can help prevent the spread of syphilis from hands to mucous membranes.

Syphilis: The Impersonator

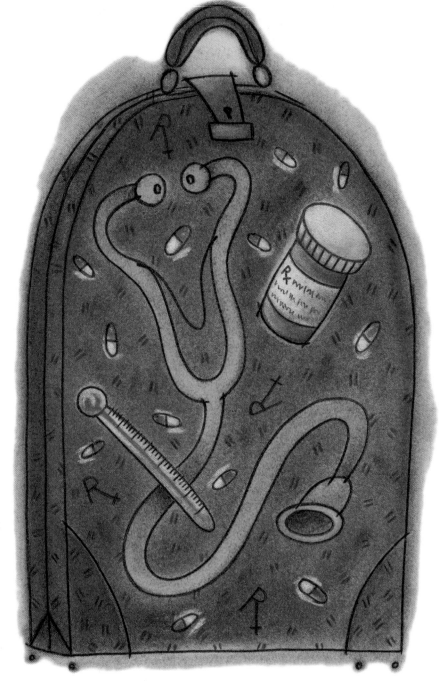

Syphilis can be easily cured in its earlier stages.

Sexually Transmitted Infections

ing the first stage, called primary syphilis, a person will usually have one or more small painless sores. This sore, called a chancre (pronounced "shanker"), usually appears anywhere from ten to ninety days after infection, often about three weeks later. It develops in the spot where the bacteria invaded the body, often on or in the penis, on the labia, or inside the vagina or cervix. A person can also get a chancre on or in their mouth if they engage in oral sex with an infected person. The chancre, as in Kristin's story, typically goes away on its own within a few weeks.

Often people do not realize they have syphilis during its first stage. Most chancres cause little or no pain. Since they usually develop in areas of the body that people do not look at closely, people can easily miss that they even have one. In fact, many chancres are on internal areas such as a man's urethra or inside a woman's vagina. Since the sores go away on their own, many people, like Kristin, do not seek medical treatment even when they notice. Although a chancre may not seem like a big deal, it is swarming with bacteria and is highly infectious. The clear liquid that seeps from the sore will spread the infection to anyone who allows it to come into contact with vulnerable parts of his body.

After the chancre heals, the bacteria enter the bloodstream, bringing on the second stage of syphilis, called secondary syphilis. When Kristin came down with her "flu bug," she was really having the first symptoms of secondary syphilis. The symptoms can include fever, headache, sore throat, achy joints, rash, swollen LYMPH NODES, patchy hair loss and sores in the genital area that look like warts. The rash is one of the more common symptoms. It does not itch and can cover the whole body or just a few places, like the soles of the feet or the palms of the hands. Many people do not seek medical attention or do not receive appropriate treatment when they do seek it because many of these symptoms are similar to those experienced with other less serious illnesses. Like syphilis's first stage, the symptoms of the second stage will go away on their own. However, the infection is still able to be passed to others even when symptoms aren't present. This stage can last as long as a year or two, with symptoms coming and going during that time.

Eventually, if the infection is not treated, it will enter the latent period. During this time, the infection is present in the body, but causes no visible signs. A person with latent syphilis can still infect other people. This time can last for months or even many years. The infected person's body is trying to fight off the infection and is successful more than half the time. About 85 percent of people beat the infection, even if they never seek treatment. However, the other 30 percent will eventually leave the latent period and have serious consequences.

The fourth stage, called tertiary syphilis, happens when the infection starts to destroy the infected person's organs. It can infect and cause serious damage to any organ system, including

Syphilis can be passed from an infected mother to her unborn baby. Unlike gonorrhea, which only infects newborns during delivery, syphilis can actually infect a fetus while it is still in its mother's body. This type of syphilis, called congenital syphilis, is the worst form of the infection. Symptoms include rash, brain damage, deformed bones or teeth, and hearing loss. Babies with syphilis, like adults, are treated with penicillin. However, the treatment is more complicated and usually requires working with a specialist. While the infection can be cured, much of the damage is permanent and will affect the child throughout his life.

Sexually Transmitted Infections

the bones, liver, skin, and heart. If it affects the brain, it is called neurosyphilis. Tertiary syphilis can cause a variety of serious consequences, including permanent damage to any number of organs, insanity, and even death.

Testing and Treatment of Syphilis

Doctors can diagnose syphilis in two different ways. The first is to take a swab from the chancre or rash, if the person has one, and to look at it under a microscope. However, the bacteria are hard to see, even under very powerful microscopes, and even a well-trained laboratory technician might miss the presence of the bacteria. The more common way of diagnosing syphilis is with a blood test that detects the immune system's response to the infection. These blood tests are cheap and easy to perform. As a result, many doctors do them as a matter of course during any complete physical, even if they have no reason to suspect the infection. However, these tests do not always work properly during the first weeks after infection, because the immune system does not always have enough of a response to be detected by the test. If doctors still suspect that a person is infected, they will repeat the tests again in several months.

Fortunately, syphilis is almost always completely curable with injections of penicillin (or other drugs if the infected person is allergic to penicillin). Unlike gonorrhea, syphilis has not become resistant to penicillin. During primary, secondary, and early latent syphilis, the infection can usually be cured with one injection of penicillin. Unfortunately, more than half of people who receive this treatment have side effects about eight hours after getting the shot, probably as a result of the rapid killing of the bacteria. These effects include a fever, chills, aches, sweating,

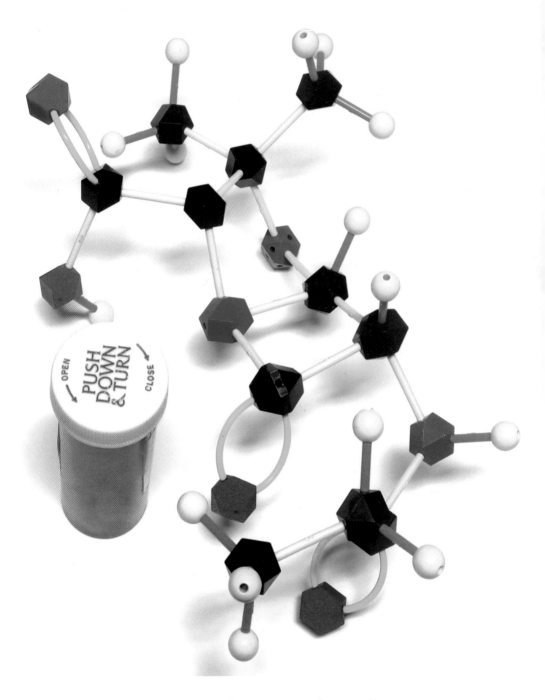

Chemical structure of penicillin.

Sexually Transmitted Infections

Syphilis was very difficult to treat in the years before doctors discovered that penicillin was effective. The treatments used poisonous metals such as mercury and were so miserable that some believed they were worse than the infection itself. The best of these treatments was called salvarsan-606, which was made from arsenic. A German scientist named Paul Ehrlich accidentally discovered the benefits of arsenic for treatment of syphilis. He was trying to cure a completely different illness, called African sleeping sickness, and tested 605 different substances before he tried salvarsan-606. It did not cure African sleeping sickness, but he discovered that it was effective against syphilis. However, arsenic is a very poisonous and unpleasant substance. In fact, it has been used throughout the centuries in books and in real life to commit many murders. Salvarsan-606 had to be given in small doses over a long period of time and caused many unpleasant side effects. However, until penicillin was discovered, it was the best treatment available.

and a worsening of the chancre or rash. Luckily, these symptoms usually go away within twenty-four hours and will not lead to any long-term problems. A person in the later stages of syphilis will probably get a weekly shot for three weeks in a row. Neurosyphilis, however, will require a stay in the hospital and IV penicillin. While the infection can be cured, any damage to organs done by the infection will not be reversed, and this serious infection can have life-long effects.

4

CHLAMYDIA:
The Strong Silent Type

Brett was excited! He had just gotten a phone call from an Air Force recruiter who was offering him a position as a fighter jet pilot. Ever since he was a little boy playing in the treehouse in the back yard he had dreamed of this day. He worked hard at school to get good grades because he knew that the Air Force only wanted the best and brightest for its pilot training school. Brett only had to pass a physical to complete the requirements for the program. The recruiter had set up an appointment for him at a local doctor's of-

fice in two weeks. He knew that would be no problem. He took good care of himself and was very healthy. Brett never missed school and had perfect vision and hearing, two more keys to being a good pilot. His eyes had bothered him some lately, but he figured that it was just a slight allergy. No big deal. He had a habit of playing with his eyelid, and thought maybe that could be part of the problem. Brett called his long-time girlfriend to tell her the great news.

As time passed, Brett's eyes got more and more irritated, but he ignored the itching and watering as much as he could. One morning, Brett woke up and his eyes were glued shut. He pried them open and went into the bathroom to clean them up and get ready for school. He noticed that his eyes were extremely irritated. He looked at himself in the mirror, noticing that his vision was slightly blurred. This worried him. He had never had blurred vision before. He called for his mother and asked her to call the family doctor. The doctor agreed to see him right away.

Brett grew more worried as they got closer to the doctor's office. His vision had not gotten clearer, and the irritation in his eyes had become a painful burning. He could barely keep his eyes open.

Brett went to see his family doctor, who ran a bunch of tests. The doctor was quite surprised when the lab technician called to say that Brett's discharge was full of the bacteria that cause chlamydia. He had known Brett all of his life and never thought he would be the type to have an STI. He called Brett right away and asked him to come in as soon as possible.

The doctor told Brett the diagnosis. Brett was shocked. He had never had sex with anyone other than his girlfriend and always with a condom. The doctor told him that would not always prevent chlamydia infections, and that it was obvious Brett should have a chat with his girlfriend. Brett's vision cleared up after he took the medicine the doctor had given him. When Brett found out his girlfriend was infected with chlamydia by another boy she had sex with a few

Sexually Transmitted Infections

months earlier, he decided to end the relationship. His only comfort was the knowledge that he was going to fly fighter jets soon.

Chlamydia is one of the most common STIs in the world. More than one million new cases occur each year in the United States alone. The good news is that it is a curable infection. The bad news is that it often goes undiagnosed for long periods of time, allowing it to cause serious damage and spread undetected among its victims. Chlamydia was the most frequently reported STI in the United States in 2011. New infections are most often reported by men and women under the age of twenty-five.

Chlamydia is usually considered a **CHRONIC** infection. It has few true warning signs, and has often been called the "Silent Syndrome" because infected people will not always display symptoms. Archaeologists have found what they believe is evidence of chlamydia in ancient Egyptian tombs, meaning that it could have been affecting humans for thousands of years.

Chlamydia is one of the most financially important STIs in the world. Treating this infection is estimated to cost in excess of twenty-four billion dollars each year in North America alone. This cost is likely to be an underestimate because many of the people that are diagnosed with gonorrhea also have chlamydia, and the drugs used to treat gonorrhea will kill the chlamydia bacteria as well.

Cause and Transmission of Chlamydia

Chlamydia is caused by an infection of the bacterium *Chlamydia trachomatis*. This bacterium prefers to live on the linings of the urethra, vagina, and cervix. It can also move into the fallopian tubes, anus and rectum, the underside of the eyelid, or the throat. It is spread by contact with the semen or

Sexually Transmitted Infections

vaginal fluid of an infected person. Chlamydia usually passes from person to person during anal or vaginal sex. It can also spread through oral sex, though this is less likely. All it takes to spread this infection is contact between infected fluids and mucous membranes. The infection transfers less easily through oral sex because the bacteria that cause it target the mucous membranes of the genital regions, not those of the mouth or throat. The bacteria are also easily spread from a woman's genital region to her anus or rectum by careless wiping with toilet paper after urination.

Infections of the eyes, like the one Brett had, are usually the result of hand-to-eye contact after contact with infected fluids, though it is possible for discharge from the penis or vagina to come directly into contact with the eyes, especially during oral sex, transferring the bacteria. Chlamydia cannot be passed by shaking hands or sitting on toilet seats, because the bacteria do not survive long outside the body.

Chlamydia can infect a newborn baby during childbirth. Sometimes newborn infants get eye or ear infections by exposure to infected tissues in the mother's reproductive system. Newborns are also at risk of developing pneumonia if they are exposed during birth and not treated. Chlamydia infections in infants can be deadly if left untreated.

Chlamydia takes its name from the Greek word chlamys, which means "around the shoulder." This describes how the bacteria appear when inside our cells. They tend to surround the cell's nucleus, which is like the cell's brain, making the area around it like a "shoulder" region. The infection then destroys the nucleus, killing the cell.

Symptoms and Complications of Chlamydia

One of the biggest problems with preventing the spread of chlamydia is that it often has no symptoms, especially in women. Around 75 percent of women and 50 percent of men do not develop any symptoms with chlamydia. The usual lack of symptoms makes it very difficult to collect accurate statistics for the numbers of new infections each year. The majority of the figures given above are estimates. Some doctors feel that the actual numbers are quite a bit higher than reported by the major health organizations because many people simply do not realize they are infected. Symptoms that do show usually start within three weeks of the exposure to the bacteria. Most major health organizations consider a person infectious from the time of infection until the end of treatment, even if he or she has no symptoms.

The typical symptoms of a chlamydia infection are often quite minor. The most common symptoms in women are pain while urinating and thick vaginal discharge. The mucus of the discharge is very infectious because it is packed full of bacteria. In men, the symptoms are similar. The most common symptoms of chlamydia in men are pain while urinating and clear milky discharge from the penis.

Several of the complications of chlamydia are the same for men, women, and children. Among these are proctitis, which is a severely swollen rectum or anus, and urethritis, or a swelling of the urethra; and conjunctivitis, which is an inflammation of the mucous membrane that lines the inner surface of the eyelid and the exposed surface of the eyeball. Each of these conditions is accompanied by pain in the affected region. Chlamydia infections of the mouth and throat are usually symptom-free. If symptoms do occur, the most common are soreness and redness in the mouth or throat.

Sexually Transmitted Infections

Women who have chlamydia often do not realize they are infected until it spreads to deeper parts of the reproductive system. The most serious problems, such as loss of fertility, arise from infection of the fallopian tubes. Some of the symptoms associated with infection of the fallopian tubes include lower back pain, pain during intercourse, spotting between menstrual periods, and nausea or fever.

Sometimes, a chlamydia infection can cause other serious problems. A condition called lymphogranuloma venereum can occur because of an untreated chlamydia infection. The result

It is possible to pass chlamydia through kissing, but it is not as likely to be passed orally as it is sexually.

Chlamydia: The Strong Silent Type

A chlamydia infection has been shown to increase the risk of becoming infected with HIV, the cause of AIDS. HIV is transmitted mainly by transfer of infected blood or other bodily fluids from person to person; the sores that arise as a result of a chlamydia infection are often hidden from view, and open sores that are oozing blood increase the risk of transmission.

of this is the opening of painful oozing sores in the genital region that often turn into scars. The sores are not limited to external parts of the body. When the sores are on internal parts of the reproductive system, the scarring can lead to infertility. They can block the tubes that transport sperm or eggs, preventing the reproductive system from working properly. Untreated chlamydial infections can also lead to pelvic inflammatory disease (PID).

When the infection affects the lining of the eyelids, a condition called conjunctivitis occurs. This can be very serious. Conjunctivitis, if not quickly treated, can cause blindness. The young man from our story, Brett, was very lucky that he was treated promptly, because his dreams of flying could have been crushed by blindness.

Testing and Treatment of Chlamydia

Detection of a chlamydia infection is done by swabbing the cervix in women and the penis in men or by testing a urine sample for traces of the bacteria. The samples are sent out to a laboratory for examination. The bacteria that cause chlamydia are easily identified using relatively inexpensive methods. Once the bacteria are identified, technicians can report the results to the doctors. Testing usually takes about one week from start to finish.

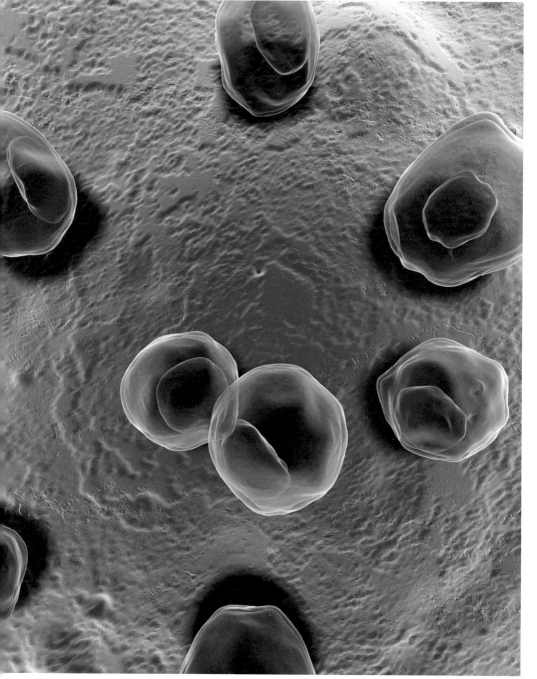

Close up of chlamydia bacteria.

Chlamydia: The Strong Silent Type

STIs like chlamydia are part of the risks of becoming an adult. Knowing how to protect yourself can save you a lot of discomfort, pain, and embarrassment.

Sexually Transmitted Infections

MYTH VERSUS FACT

MYTH: Once you have had chlamydia, you cannot get it again.

FACT: Having had chlamydia does not make you any less likely to get it a second (or a third or a fourth . . .) time.

Luckily, chlamydia is treatable with antibiotics. The standard drugs used to remove the infection are azithromycin (Zithromax®) and doxycycline. Other antibiotics are also effective, but are used less often because they have more severe side effects. The symptoms of gonorrhea and chlamydia are very similar, so doctors often treat for both, because the cost of treatment is lower than the cost of testing. The CDC actually recommends combining the treatments because of the similarity of symptoms and the likelihood that infected persons would have both gonorrhea and chlamydia.

Typically, a standard course of antibiotics will quickly clear up a chlamydia infection. It is usually very responsive to the medications used to treat it. Once the infection is cleared, the sores will heal like any other wound. Women whose sexual partners have not been treated expose themselves to a high risk of reinfection because their systems are vulnerable. Reinfection increases the risk of serious complications like sterility and PID.

5

HERPES:
The Bad Houseguest

Laura and Jason had been going out ever since the junior prom last spring. Most of their classmates agreed that they were the senior class's cutest couple. They were both good kids with big plans for their lives; Jason wanted to go to medical school, and Laura wanted to be a lawyer or maybe an architect. They spent every spare moment they could together, but they never let it get in the way of their studies.

They had both been in relationships before, but nothing as serious as this. Although their physical relationship had intensified, they had talked about sex and decided not to take the risk. Laura and Jason both knew about the dangers of pregnancy and STIs, and neither one wanted anything to interfere with their plans. That, however, did not mean that they were completely avoiding sexual intimacy. Laura had heard the term "outercourse" used to describe everything but intercourse, and she thought that was a pretty good description of what they did.

Laura had been having trouble with bladder infections for the last six months or so. Each time, her family doctor would give her an antibiotic and she would feel better after a few days. One time, she also had a little blister that she noticed when she was going to the bathroom, but that cleared up with the antibiotic. Her best friend suggested it could be an STI, but Laura knew it couldn't be. Although Jason had been sexually active before they got together, she was a virgin.

The third time she went to the doctor for her bladder infection, he asked her more questions than he had in the past. She ended up describing the blister, which had reappeared. He insisted on taking a swab of it and sending it out for testing.

When she went back a few days later, the doctor told her she had genital herpes. She tried to tell him it was impossible, that she had never had sex. He explained to her that she could definitely have gotten herpes without having intercourse, and she would have it for the rest of her life. He told her it was really common, but that didn't make her feel any better. She was completely grossed out and humiliated!

Although genital herpes usually has relatively mild symptoms and few complications, it continues to be one of the most dreaded STIs, because it has no cure. Once people are infected with herpes, they will have it for the rest of their lives. According to the CDC, one out of every six people over the age of four-

HERPES: *The Bad Houseguest*

teen in the United States has genital herpes, though many of them do not know it.

Causes, Symptoms, and Complications of Herpes

Genital herpes is caused by a virus called herpes simplex (HSV). Once the herpes virus enters the body, like a bad houseguest, it never leaves. As explained in chapter 1, there are few antiviral drugs. Scientists have not been able to find a cure for herpes at this point, though some antiviral drugs help keep the infection under control. However, much of the time, the virus is latent or inactive. The viruses in a person with genital herpes spend most of their time in the nerve cells along the lower spinal cord.

The best-known symptom of genital herpes is the characteristic blisters that form on or around the genitals or anus. These outbreaks occur when the virus travels up the nerves from its normal resting place near the spinal cord and comes to the surface in an area serviced by that particular nerve group (which includes the entire pubic region, the anal region, lower buttocks, and inner thighs). The blisters are usually about the size of a pinhead, though they can be larger. An infected person may have just one or a cluster of blisters. They are red, bubbled, and often itchy or painful. They typically burst and form painful ulcers that ooze virus-rich fluid.

The sores will typically appear about ten days to two weeks from the time of infection, if they appear at all. Many people with genital herpes have no symptoms and are never aware they have the virus. However, for the people who have outbreaks, the first one is usually the worst. After the blisters burst, they will start to heal. If the blisters are on skin surfaces, they will scab over and eventually dry up and fall off. If, however, they are on moist mucous membrane areas, they will not scab over.

Sexually Transmitted Infections

There are two types of herpes: HSV-1 and HSV-2. Although they are different viruses, they cause similar symptoms. HSV-2 commonly causes infection around the genital or anal region, and HSV-1 usually infects the area around the mouth, causing cold sores. However, either virus can infect any part of the body, and genital herpes can be caused by either type of virus. These viruses are quite similar to the ones that cause chicken pox and mononucleosis.

People who have a symptomatic outbreak soon after infection can expect to have many more outbreaks in the years to come (typically four or five a year). Luckily, the number of outbreaks usually decreases as time goes on and the body becomes better at fighting the virus.

Other symptoms can occur, especially during the first episode. They can include flu-like symptoms (fever, swollen glands, nausea, chills, fatigue, etc.), a second crop of blisters, painful urination, weakness or pain in the lower back, legs, genitals or buttocks, discharge in women, or numbness in the genitals or lower back. Most people with HSV-2 infections have no symptoms or such mild symptoms that they do not even recognize them, instead mistaking them for insect bites or other mild rashes.

Herpes usually has a "warning period" before an outbreak of blisters, called the prodrome period. People with the infection will experience itching, burning, or tingling of their skin in the area that is about to have blisters. They may also have a bump or a reddening of the skin in that area. Other people will have no warning at all and go straight into the syndrome period, during which they suffer from the blisters and other symptoms.

HERPES: The Bad Houseguest

73

When people do not practice monogamous sex, herpes can pass easily from person to person, infecting large groups.

Sexually Transmitted Infections

Although herpes outbreaks can be quite unpleasant, they all pass on their own, without medication. The first herpes outbreak tends to have the worst symptoms and takes the longest to heal, often two to four weeks (and sometimes as much six weeks). Later outbreaks are typically five to seven days long, though they can certainly be much longer.

The severity of outbreaks varies from person to person. Of course, some people have no outbreaks at all, and others have mild symptoms they do not even recognize. Still other people, however, have very painful and disruptive outbreaks that cause them to miss school or work. Symptoms tend to be more severe in women than in men. People with conditions that weaken their **IMMUNE SYSTEMS**, such as HIV or AIDS, usually have more frequent and longer outbreaks.

Many people who have herpes mistake it for other conditions. Those with milder symptoms may believe they have an insect bite. Other people might believe they are having an allergic reaction or irritation from spermicides or soap, which could cause itching and bumps. A woman who has a discharge might think she has a **YEAST INFECTION**, treat it with over-the-counter medication, and believe the treatment successful when the symptoms go away. Painful urination sometimes leads people, like Laura in our story, to believe they have bladder infections.

Sometimes herpes can have more serious complications, though this is quite rare. One such complication is viral meningitis, swelling in the lining of the spinal cord. Although this is rarely life-threatening, it can cause neck aches and pain in the eyes when looking at light and can make people quite sick. Herpes is most serious when passed from a mother to a fetus or a newborn baby. Many of these newborns will suffer permanent brain damage or even death. In addition, like chlamydia, herpes plays a role in the spread of HIV, because its open sores make

HERPES: The Bad Houseguest

it easier for an infected person to get HIV or transmit it if they already have it.

Transmission of Herpes

Herpes is transmitted by contact with an area that is infected, especially when there is an open blister, or with bodily fluids that are infected, like semen, vaginal fluids, or even the saliva (or spit) of a person who has an oral herpes infection. The areas that are in the greatest danger of being infected are the moist mucous membranes, like the mouth, eye, or genital skin. However, the virus can enter the body through any place where the skin is broken. Women are more likely to get genital herpes than men, because they have a larger moist mucous membrane area than men.

The virus does not last long outside the body, since it will become inactive as soon as the fluid it is in dries. This means that it is extremely unlikely to be passed on toilet seats or towels.

Obviously, a person in the midst of a herpes outbreak is highly infectious. A person in the prodrome (or warning) period is also infectious. In addition, however, the virus can be transmitted when the infected person is having no symptoms whatsoever. Sometimes the virus will travel to the surface of the skin and cause no symptoms. At those times, the virus can be passed to other people. Many transmissions of herpes occur when people are not aware they are infectious.

Although condoms are a very smart precaution and will reduce the likelihood of getting infected with herpes, they certainly do not prevent all herpes infections. Herpes blisters are often in areas that are not covered by condoms, or virus-rich bodily fluids may come into contact with the skin regardless of condom use.

Sexually Transmitted Infections

MYTH VERSUS FACT

MYTH: You can get herpes from sharing a hot tub or swimming pool with an infected person.

FACT: Herpes cannot be transmitted by sharing a hot tub or swimming pool with an infected person (unless you have sexual contact with that person).

As mentioned previously, herpes can be passed from mother to child either before birth (especially if the mother gets the infection for the first time while pregnant) or during the birth process if the mother has sores during delivery.

Testing and Treatment of Herpes

Many doctors will be able to recognize the characteristic herpes blister if they have the opportunity to examine it during an outbreak. Of course, this diagnosis would have to be confirmed with other testing. The fluid from swabbing or scraping an active blister can be tested if the person is in the midst of an outbreak. Blood tests can diagnose herpes whether or not the person is having any symptoms at that time.

As stated earlier, no cure is available for herpes at this time. Once a person is infected, he will be infected for the rest of his life. However, the last twenty or twenty-five years have seen the introduction of antiviral drugs that can often prevent symptoms from occurring and lessen their severity when they do occur. The first of these drugs was acyclovir (sold as Zovirax®),

Herpes virus.

Sexually Transmitted Infections

which keeps the virus from reproducing. It can be applied as a cream, which shortens the length of time it takes for blisters to heal, or taken as a pill, which makes outbreaks come less often and be less severe in people who have frequent and painful outbreaks. Unfortunately, however, acyclovir is like antibiotics and does not work as well when it has been used many times.

Luckily, newer drugs that work in essentially the same way have been developed. In clinical studies, famcyclovir (sold as Famvir®) and valacyclovir (sold as Valtrex®) have been more effective than acyclovir at preventing outbreaks and making them shorter when they occur. People who have frequent and severe outbreaks can take them all the time, and people who have less severe herpes can take them just when they feel an outbreak coming on. Valtrex® has also been approved for the purpose of reducing the risk of an infected person passing the infection to their sexual partners. Although herpes is not life-threatening, it is a very serious infection with serious consequences for infected people.

HERPES: The Bad Houseguest

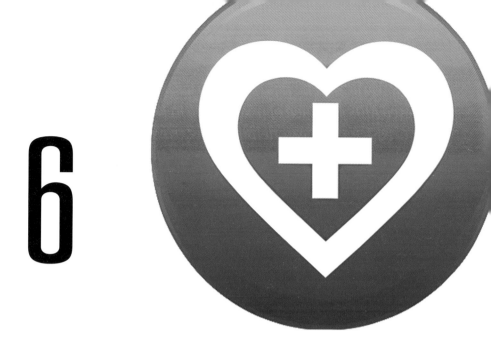

6

HIV/AIDS:
The International Bad Boy

Greg worked as a flight attendant for a major international airline in the late 1970s and early 1980s. He loved his job; after all, no other job allowed a person to see the world and get paid for the travel. The best part was that he got plenty of ground time in all the cities the airline visited—and he met hundreds of women from all over the world. Greg was a very sexually active young man and bragged about his lifestyle constantly. He did not practice safe *sex, however, and he paid a high price for his poor decisions. He contracted AIDS and died of pneumonia in 1986.*

Greg kept a diary detailing his travels and exploits (including those with women) over the years. Using this diary, international health organization researchers were able to follow the trail of infection left by Greg and the women he slept with. The researchers believe that Greg had unprotected sex with around forty women. Thirty-three of them have since died of AIDS. The others were lucky and did not get infected. Each of the women were sexually active and had contact with other men over the years. In the end, the researchers concluded that at least six hundred people were infected as a result of the behaviors of Greg and his friends. Many of them have died.

AIDS is a very serious problem around the world. No nation has escaped the touch of this deadly disease. Areas like Africa and India are particularly hard hit because they lack the technology and money to fight the spread of the disease. Having money and technology, however, is not the miracle answer to stopping AIDS. All the developed nations of the world are currently struggling to contain this disease, and few are having true success. According to Avert, an international HIV/AIDS charity, in 2010, 2.7 million adults and 390,000 children were newly infected with HIV. Approximately 2 million adults and children died of AIDS during that same period. Since AIDS is currently incurable, the focus of the fight has historically been on prevention. Several drugs that can slow the development of AIDS have been discovered, but there is currently no way to remove the virus from an infected individual.

The first reported cases of AIDS in North America occurred in 1981. It is now commonly believed by scientists that this disease originated in Africa because the virus that causes it closely resembles immunodeficiency viruses that affect monkeys and apes. HIV may have evolved from one of these viruses. The most

Romantic relationships are exciting and fun—but they should also be safe.

widely accepted theory for how people came into contact with the virus is that people killed and ate an infected chimpanzee. It is clear from detailed scientific examination that the virus existed well before it was documented in North America. Tissue samples of several people that died young in the 1950s and 1960s tested positive for HIV. There is evidence that the virus first jumped to humans in the late 1940s or early 1950s.

The virus spread slowly at first, restricted to small areas of the world. In the 1970s and 1980s, aided by increasing international travel and the rapid growth of low-technology blood donations, the virus began to spread across the world, achieving pandemic, or worldwide, status. Sexually active travelers, like Greg, could pick up the disease in foreign countries and spread it at the speed of an airliner to other nations. The establishment of blood banks and medical associations like the Red Cross made transfusions of blood common in hospitals around the world. Blood was not screened as carefully as it is now, allowing HIV infected blood to be transfused into medical patients. Another factor in the spread of HIV was the increase of drug use that occurred in the 1970s. Following the Vietnam War, use of drugs that had to be injected grew rapidly, and so did needle sharing among drug users.

Cause and Transmission of HIV and AIDS

AIDS stands for acquired immune deficiency syndrome. The disease is caused by an infection with the human immunodeficiency virus (HIV). There are two major types of HIV that have been identified, HIV-1 and HIV-2. Most cases of AIDS worldwide are caused by HIV-1, which is more easily spread than HIV-2. At least ten different forms of HIV-1 exist around the world. Each has different characteristics. The existence of these differing forms allows doctors and scientists to determine where the virus causing a particular infection originated.

The virus is easily passed from person to person in bodily fluids, including semen, blood, and vaginal fluids. The most common ways the virus spreads are through unprotected sex and needle sharing by drug users, though we should be concerned about other methods as well. An infected mother easily passes the virus to her unborn baby during pregnancy, though certain drug treatments can reduce the risk to the child if they are used properly. It is also possible for a mother to pass HIV through her breast milk. HIV is so good at infecting people that all it takes to start a deadly infection is one single virus particle! This makes it possible for the virus to spread through invisible blood cells on a used needle. Tattoo parlors have received some attention for spreading HIV by not properly cleaning their equipment.

Splashing of blood, vaginal fluid, or semen from an infected person on unbroken skin will not pass the infection. If the fluid gets into a body opening such as the nose or eye, it can cause

MYTH VERSUS FACT

MYTH: It is not safe to be close to someone with HIV or AIDS.

TRUTH: This virus is not passed through casual contact such as hand shaking or hugging. There are very few reported cases of HIV passage through kissing, and those cases involved people with bleeding gums or open sores in the mouth. Kissing is generally considered safe behavior. HIV does not pass from person to person through the air like a flu or cold. It cannot be spread by coughing or sneezing.

infection by entering the body through the soft tissues of the mucous membranes there. Anyone who comes into contact with bodily fluids should promptly wash the affected surface to avoid getting it into vulnerable areas, if it has not already.

HIV makes us sick by attacking the cells of our immune system. The virus attaches itself to certain cells called CD4+ T cells, which just happen to be very important in our bodies' response to viruses. It takes over the cell and forces it to create more cop-

If you choose to tattoo or pierce, be sure to use safe tattoo and piercing parlors to avoid exposing yourself to the HIV virus.

Sexually Transmitted Infections

ies of the virus. One virus can infect one cell and cause the production of hundreds more viruses, able to attack one cell each. The viruses produced inside the cell burst out into the blood, killing the cell in the process.

Symptoms and Complications of HIV and AIDS

Infection by the virus is usually followed by a short flu-like illness that passes quickly. The virus then enters a latent period between the time of initial infection and the beginning of additional symptoms. The latent period can last many years. Some people have had latency last as long as fifteen years. The average length of latency for HIV infection is eight years. During this time, the lack of early warning signs allows the virus to spread undetected through a population. People in early stages of the infection usually look and feel completely normal. As time passes, the virus grows in number in the bloodstream.

One of the first clues to the existence of HIV was a sudden increase in a very rare form of cancer known as Kaposi's sarcoma. This cancer was known to occur mainly in older people but started being diagnosed in young, gay males about 1981. This prompted scientists to look for reasons for the sudden change. They noticed that other diseases were on the rise among gay males, such as pneumonia, and began looking for answers. The search ended with the discovery of HIV-1. Since then, Kaposi's sarcoma has become one of the warning signs for HIV infection. It causes open sores on the skin that usually become infected and will not heal.

As the virus spreads, and more and more of the immune cells are attacked and killed, the body becomes less able to fight off other infections. People whose immune systems are weakened by HIV become very vulnerable to all infections and eventually develop AIDS. The disease we call AIDS is actually the end

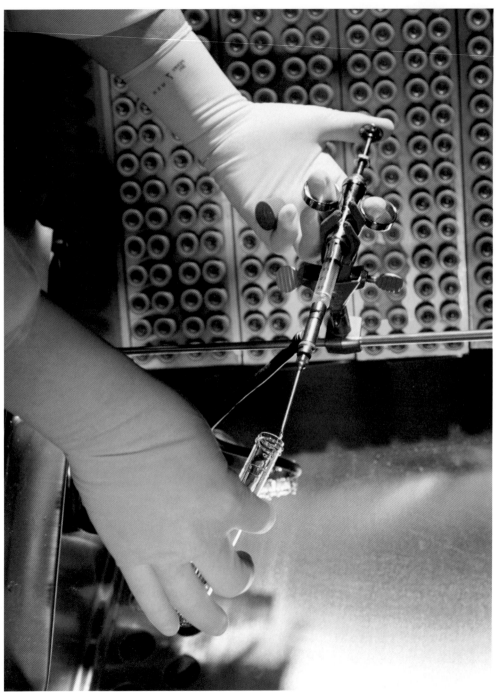

Researchers are looking for a cure for HIV and AIDS.

Sexually Transmitted Infections

stage of the HIV infection. A person with advanced AIDS could actually die from infections that most people are able to easily fight off. This is because some of the most important parts of the immune system have been taken over and destroyed by the virus. This is a condition called immunosuppression. Since the immune system is our main defense against infection and some types of cancers, immunosuppression is often fatal.

During immunosuppression, people are very vulnerable to diseases that do not usually cause severe distress. Illnesses that we normally consider minor inconveniences become far more serious. A common cold can be deadly. The infections that attack immunosuppressed people are known as **OPPORTUNISTIC INFECTIONS**. These are the actual causes of death in AIDS patients. HIV does not kill. Instead, it severely weakens the immune system, leaving people unable to fight off other diseases. The most common cause of death among AIDS patients is pneumonia caused by a parasite that infects the lungs. Greg, our young flight attendant, died of such a disease. Most people are routinely exposed and easily fight off the infection. AIDS patients die from it.

Opportunistic infections can be caused by viruses, bacteria, protists, or fungi. Effective treatments exist for all but the viral infections. AIDS patients usually take a wide range of medications to extend their lives as long as possible, but sooner or later, an infection will take hold and they will be unable to survive. As

HIV attacks a cell vital to the immune system, called a T-lymphocyte. These are the cells that attack and destroy invaders in our bodies. Without them, we are far less able to fight off even minor infections. A common cold can actually be deadly to a person without lymphocytes. This is what makes AIDS the killer it is.

HIV/AIDS: The International Bad Boy

time passes, they grow weak from the constant battle raging in their bodies.

Testing and Treatment for HIV and AIDS

One of the two ways to detect an HIV infection is a blood test that looks for specific types of cells called antibodies that are released by the immune system in response to an infection. The other is also a blood test that looks for proteins that are produced early in the infection by cells with HIV attached to them. The proteins are called P24 antigens and can be detected much more quickly in the blood than antibodies. An antigen test can identify an infection within about a month after infection has entered the body, while the antibody test usually is only accurate after a longer period of time, sometimes as long as six months.

These tests require a period of time to have passed between the time of infection and the time of the test. Since HIV is incurable and slow to progress, there is less emphasis on detecting the infection quickly. The issue with not being able to detect an infection is only truly important when the infected person's behaviors put others at risk.

A few key tests can also determine how well developed an infection is in HIV positive individuals. These tests are used to schedule the beginning of drug treatments designed to slow

AIDS is not the only disease that causes immunosuppression. Some forms of cancer like leukemia may result in this condition as well. The parts of the immune system that protect us from illness or infection can be damaged by the treatments for these diseases.

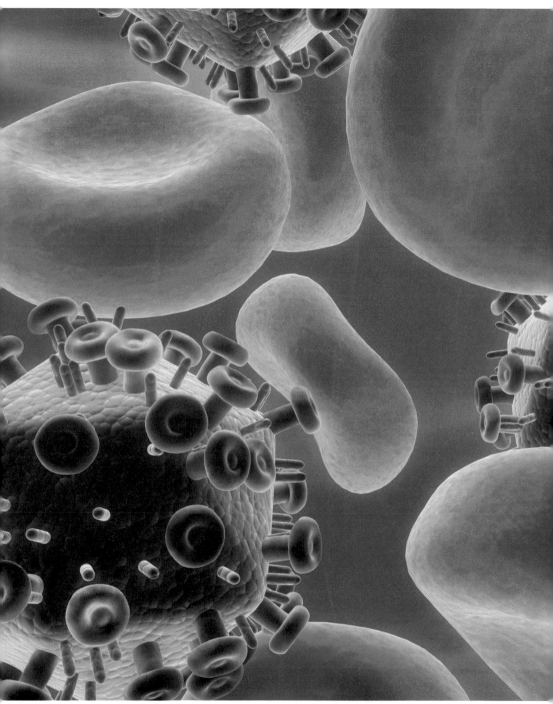

HIV virus in the bloodstream.

HIV/AIDS: The International Bad Boy

One of the most commonly prescribed medications for fighting the progression of AIDS is called Retrovir® or AZT. Most combinations of drugs prescribed contain this medication because it has shown the most promise in slowing the disease. It is not often given alone since HIV-1 has rapidly developed resistance to the effects of this drug when it is not combined with others.

the advance of the infection. One of the main methods of determining the degree of HIV infection is called a viral load test. This test determines the approximate number of viral particles in the blood. The number of particles can be used to track the progress of the infection to the end stage. Once a certain number of viral particles are detected, the general policy is to start drug treatments to slow the infection. Another method commonly used is the CD4+ test. This counts the number of CD4+ cells in the blood. Since the virus attacks and destroys these cells, a count of the number in the blood can give an estimate of how bad the infection is. A low number of CD4+ cells means many virus particles are attacking the immune system. When a person's CD4+ cell count drops below a certain number, drug therapy is begun.

The fact that a virus causes AIDS is one of the main reasons we have not yet been able to cure it. Scientists have found very few medicines that can kill viruses, because viruses do not always behave like living creatures. Viruses only reproduce when they are inside cells, so they are very difficult to kill. Our immune systems can "learn" to recognize and destroy viruses, but the virus that causes AIDS attacks and kills the very cells that would destroy it. As more and more of the immune cells are killed off, our immune systems become weaker and weaker.

Sexually Transmitted Infections

Prescription medications can slow the progression of AIDS symptoms.

HIV/AIDS: The International Bad Boy

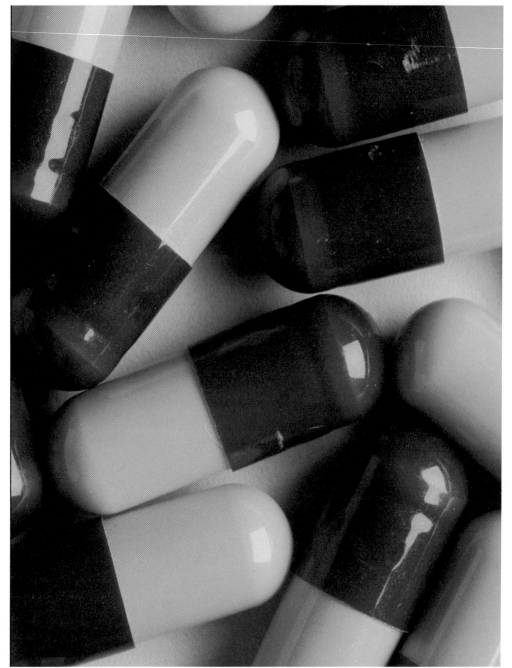

Although there is no cure for AIDS, some medications can slow down the disease. However, these drugs are hard on the liver.

Among the treatments that do exist, a few have been very promising. Unfortunately, the virus evolves relatively rapidly and is capable of developing resistance to antiviral drugs over the course of several months. This makes it very hard to stop with traditional drug therapy. Currently, about twenty antiretroviral drugs are commonly used to fight HIV infection. Most often, they are used in combination, because each has a different mode of action against the virus. Combining several drugs in one therapy has been shown to be the most effective method for slowing the progress of AIDS.

The drugs used to treat an HIV infection are very powerful medicine. They usually have some severe side effects that can have great impact on the quality of life for the patient. Many AIDS patients report chronic fatigue, weight loss, **MUSCLE WASTING**, and nausea as a result of their medications. The drugs put a large strain on the heart and liver of the patient as well. Some AIDS patients die from liver failure well before the disease destroys their immune system, because the liver filters the waste products of the many drugs from the blood. One of the most disturbing side effects of the treatments is a feeling of severe pain over large areas of the body as the medications affect the nervous system.

The treatments currently available have little possibilty of curing the disease. Research is ongoing, with the hope that someday soon we will be able to stop AIDS once and for all. The best bet right now is to control or stop the behaviors that expose us to risk of infection. Condom use during sex and using only fresh needles during drug use can help slow the spread.

7

The Rest of the Gang

Although the STIs addressed in chapters 2 through 7 are some of the most significant players in the world of STIs, there are certainly a variety of other members of the gang.

Trichomaniasis

Trichomoniasis, or "trick," is a common STI that can be unpleasant but not terribly dangerous. According to the CDC, about seven million new cases occur each year in the United States. It is especially common in young, sexually active women.

Adolescence is the time of life when many people begin exploring relationships with the opposite sex. Be sure to stay safe in the process!

Sexually Transmitted Infections

The infection is caused by a microscopic protist called *Trichomonas vaginalis*. This protist usually infects the vagina in women and the urethra in men. It passes from person to person during sexual contact between genitals. Even people who have no symptoms can pass the infection to other people. Luckily, a single dose of a prescription drug, metronidazole, can cure trichomoniasis very easily. The organism is quite easy for trained laboratory technicians or doctors to recognize under a microscope, so additional tests are not usually necessary to diagnose the infection.

Symptoms usually develop within five to twenty-eight days after being infected with trichomoniasis, if they develop at all. Most men with the infection do not have any symptoms, though some do have irritation in their penis, burning after urinating or ejaculating, or small amounts of discharge. If symptoms do appear, they will sometimes disappear on their own after a few weeks, even though the man is still infected. Women, on the other hand, usually have symptoms, which can include bubbly green or gray discharge with a strong smell, pain during intercourse and urination, and irritation or itching in the genital area.

Trichomoniasis does not cause serious complications on its own, though it can result in low birth weight babies when a woman is infected during her pregnancy. However, the most serious problem associated with the infection is that it can increase the likelihood that an infected person will transmit or become infected with HIV. The genital irritation caused in women can create more places for the virus to enter the body. Men with HIV and trichomoniasis have significantly more HIV virus in their semen than men with HIV alone, which could make them more likely to infect their sexual partners.

Chancroid

Chancroid is an STI caused by *Haemophilus ducreyi*, a bacterium that was discovered in 1889. It is a highly contagious infection that causes painful ulcers on or around the genitals. In addition, it sometimes causes painful swelling of the lymph nodes that are near the genitals. It has become more common in North America over the past several years, perhaps because of an increase in immigration from Africa, where it is a very common infection.

The infection is transmitted by direct skin contact with a sore or by contact with the pus emitted by a sore. There appears to be little danger of infecting a baby during delivery, even when the mother has active sores. Those infected with chancroid are only considered infectious when they have open sores.

Symptoms of chancroid usually begin to appear within ten days of the exposure. Some patients have reported symptoms in as little as three days. The sores begin as tender bumps on the surface of the skin. The bumps become pus-filled and burst open. The sores are usually soft to the touch. Most often, the sores are very painful in men, but less in women because of the differences in the arrangement of nerve endings between the sexes. In fact, women are sometimes unaware they have been infected. After the sores develop, the lymph nodes may begin to swell on either side of the groin.

Chancroid can only be properly diagnosed by identifying the bacteria in a laboratory. The sores are often confused with syphilis or herpes symptoms. A swab of the pus can be sent to a lab for testing, and results will take several days. Once the diagnosis is made, a course of antibiotics can be prescribed. The bacteria usually respond quickly to medication. The most commonly prescribed antibiotic for chancroid is azithromycin, but other antibiotics will also kill the bacteria. The sores stop

Sexually Transmitted Infections

Antibiotics can help control the spread of chancroids from person to person.

growing shortly after beginning treatment. The time required for the sores to fully heal depends largely on the person. Sometimes, the sores will leave large areas of scar tissue.

Chancroid has few long-term health effects, but like chlamydia and herpes, has been found to increase the risk of HIV transmission. If the sores grow in areas that need to stretch, the replacement of regular skin with scar tissue can cause some problems. The swelling of the lymph nodes can sometimes result in a blockage of the glands in the node, which may result in the need for surgery to clear the blockage, restore the function of the gland, and relieve pain. The bacteria have not been found to cause any other internal problems in men or women.

Hepatitis B

Hepatitis B (HBV) is a viral infection that affects the liver. It is considered an STI because it can be transmitted by exchange of

Once Hepatitis B infects the bloodstream, there is no way to remove it.

Sexually Transmitted Infections

infected bodily fluids during unprotected sex. It affects all age groups, and sometimes causes severe liver disease or cancer. It can be fatal in some cases. Like many other viruses, once it gets into the bloodstream, it is there for life; there is no cure. Preventing people from getting infected is the only way to stop its spread. According to the CDC, about 43,000 people were newly infected with HBV in the United States in 2007.

Approximately one in twenty people in North America will get infected with HBV at some time during their lives. Those who are at the greatest risk of being infected are the people who have unprotected sex, share needles, live in a house with someone who is infected, or work in jobs that expose them to bodily fluids like blood or saliva.

The virus is relatively tough and has been known to remain infectious after long periods of time outside of the body. If an infected person spits on a surface and does not properly clean up, there will be infectious viral particles on the surface that can be picked up by the next person to touch that surface. This is one reason why people that live with HBV infected people are at risk of infection.

The symptoms of HBV infection are not always easily detected. About 40 percent of infected people do not report any symptoms. The people who do not show symptoms are called

The first hepatitis B vaccine was actually a sample of heat-killed virus taken from an infected person and grown in a set of blood samples. Injecting the dead virus into an uninfected person's body causes the immune system to produce cells that target the virus and destroy it before it can cause damage. Newer vaccines are genetically engineered in laboratories and do not use any cells or virus particles from infected individuals.

The Rest of the Gang

carriers, because they carry the infection and can transmit it, but have no obvious warning signs of the infection. Some people live their whole lives without knowing they are infected. In people who do experience symptoms, the most common are nausea, fever, vomiting, and stomach or other pain. Some people suffer from extreme fatigue and appetite loss. In severe cases, the infection can cause liver failure and lead to jaundice, a buildup of toxins in the blood, leading to yellowish skin and eyes or even death.

There is no way to cure an HBV infection, but it can be relatively easy to prevent one. There is a widely available vaccine that can prevent an individual from being infected. The vaccine does not use heat-killed or weakened viral particles like previous vaccines did, so there is no risk of infection from the vaccine. It is very safe and can protect a person for life from the virus.

Pubic Lice (Crabs)

Pubic lice, or "crabs," are an infestation of tiny crab-like PARASITES. They cling to pubic hair and feed on human blood. The scientific name of the small parasite is Pthirus pubis. Crabs are actually lice, closely related to those that are commonly found on the head. Crabs can attach not only to pubic hair, but also to other coarse body hair, such as the hair of the armpits, beard, eyelashes, eyebrows, and chest.

The life cycle of these lice has three phases. Each phase must be completed on a human host, because the crabs cannot survive more than twenty-four hours off of a body. The first phase is the egg, which is also known as a nit. When the egg hatches into a nymph, or larva, the second phase of the life cycle begins. The larva continues to develop, eventually entering the last phase of the life cycle, or the adult, crab-like phase.

Sexually Transmitted Infections

Crabs are most often transmitted by direct contact between body parts with coarse hair on them. Usually, they are transmitted during sexual contact. Crabs can be transferred nonsexually as well, though this is far less common. Remember, they can only survive for about twenty-four hours without a human host, so it is possible but unlikely to get them from infested sheets on a bed, towels, clothing, or, extremely rarely, toilet seats.

The most noticeable symptom of a crab infestation is itching around the affected area. This is a result of an allergic reaction to the saliva that the crabs inject when they bite, which contains chemicals that prevent blood from clotting so they can get a full meal from a single bite. Sometimes the bites are severe enough to cause bruising, or "blue spots."

Finding a crab infestation is relatively simple. They are tiny but visible to the naked eye, so you can see them if you look closely. They look like the crabs you might see on a beach, shrunk to the size of the period at the end of this sentence.

Adult crabs start laying their eggs almost immediately after getting their first meal from a host. One louse can lay hundreds of eggs in a short period of time. The eggs look like tiny pearls attached to the bases of the hairs.

Treatment of crabs uses either a cream or a shampoo that kills the adults, nymphs, and nits. Sometimes doctors recommend shaving the affected area to be sure that nits are removed. Using a specially designed comb also gets rid of nits.

When beginning treatment, it is very important to wash all the clothing, towels, and bed sheets that had been used during the time of the infestation in very hot (130° F/54° C or higher) water. It is not usually necessary to treat furniture. It is also important to notify all sex partners.

Crabs are a nuisance, but they have few lasting side effects. They typically just cause discomfort from the itching caused by the bites, though a person can get an infection from scratching with dirty hands.

Human Papillomavirus (HPV)

Human papillomavirus, or HPV (not to be confused with hepatitis B, often called HBV), is an extremely common and potentially serious STI. There are more than one hundred different strains of virus that fall within the category of HPV, and more that thirty of them are sexually transmitted, infecting the genital area of men and women. Many people use the term "HPV" interchangeably with "genital warts." However, while HPV does cause genital warts, most strains do not cause warts or any symptoms at all.

According to the U.S. CDC and the Canadian CIDPC, HPV is a very common STI in these countries. The CDC reports that at least half of all sexually active people in the United States get this infection at some point during the course of their lives. A staggering 80 percent of American women will have gotten a genital HPV infection by the time they reach age fifty.

Most people with genital HPV infections are completely unaware that they are infected. More than 95 percent of people with HPV do not have any visible symptoms at all. The only real symptom of HPV infection is the growth of warts. In women, genital warts usually appear on or near the labia, inside the vagina, on the cervix, or around the anus. In men, the warts typically appear near the tip of the penis. Genital warts have been known to develop in the mouth of a person who has had oral sex with an infected individual. They often appear in bunches and if left untreated usually begin to take on a cauliflower-like appearance.

HPV infections are most often diagnosed by direct observation of the warts. Sometimes, doctors will apply vinegar to areas

of suspected infection. The vinegar will cause the area that has invisible warts to appear white while the normal skin around it will remain flesh colored. Women that have been diagnosed with genital warts should also be examined for warts on the cervix, which can be done by collecting a sample of tissue from the cervix and examining it or by a test called a Pap smear. Each of these tests looks for evidence of HPV infected cells.

HPV is most often transmitted by direct physical contact with a developed wart. Some people who do not know they are infected will transmit HPV even though they do not have symptoms.

At times, genital warts will disappear without treatment. When they do not, there are a number of treatment options, depending on the size, location, and number of warts. Warts are sometimes removed from the skin using liquid nitrogen, lasers, electric irons, acid or other toxic chemicals.

Some types of HPV infection have been shown to increase the risk of certain types of cancers. For the most part, the types of HPV that cause external raised warts are considered low risk for development of cancers. The types of HPV that affect the cervix are considered high risk. The development of cancer can be prevented if women get regular Pap smears, because the pre-cancerous cells can be easily detected in this way, and treatment can be started. As a result, most doctors recommend yearly Pap smears for all women.

The treatments for genital warts can remove the external signs of infection but cannot remove the virus from the bloodstream. The warts can reappear at any time. There are medications that can be used to reduce the risk of future outbreaks, such as a drug known as alpha interferon.

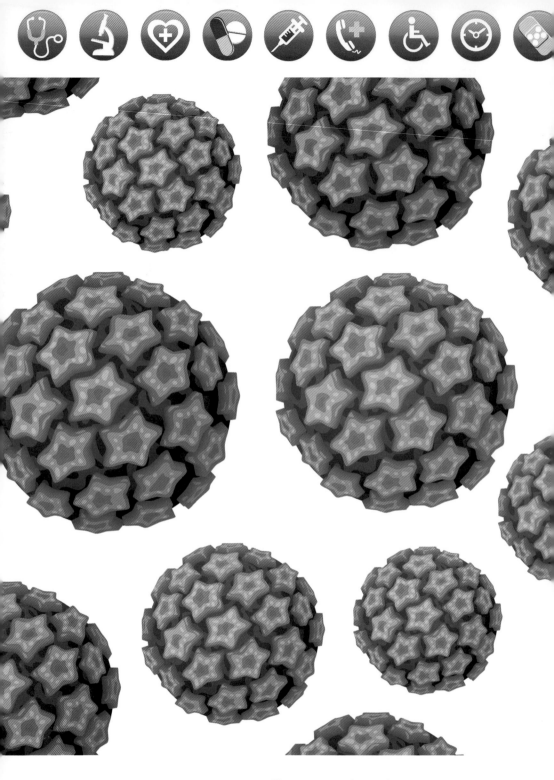

Human papillomavirus (HPV)

Sexually Transmitted Infections

Most people carry some form of the human papillomavirus in their system. Approximately a third of those strains infect the genital area, while the remaining two thirds affect other areas of the body. If you have ever had a wart on your hand or foot, you probably carry the human papillomavirus. Typically, the strains which cause warts on your hands only cause warts on hands, and the types that cause warts on your feet only cause warts on feet. You should not have to worry about spreading them to your genitals.

Obviously, STI "gang members" are a wide and varied group. You may think they are a "gross" or "yucky" topic to think about. But as you become a young adult, it only makes sense to be aware of what's out there in the world you will be encountering. Then you can make informed decisions about how to take care of yourself.

The Rest of the Gang

109

8

Playing It Safe:
Preventing STIs

Rob shifted uncomfortably in his chair under his father's gaze. He could feel his face burning. His father cleared his throat and starting talking again, "Rob, I know you hate talking about this stuff, but it's really important that you make good choices and are honest with me. You'd tell me if you were having sex, wouldn't you?"

Rob nodded, his face turning an even brighter shade of red.

His father continued, "I would rather you waited, but if you're not going to, I really want you to be careful. I have condoms right here. Do you need any?"

Rob shook his head. He felt badly about lying to his father, but he just couldn't bring himself to admit that he'd started sleeping with his girlfriend just a few weeks before. He knew he could get condoms at the clinic downtown or at the drugstore, if he could be brave enough. Unfortunately, neither he nor his girlfriend had been brave enough before, and he was awfully afraid he wouldn't be brave enough next time.

Many people, young and old, feel uncomfortable talking about sex. Unfortunately, the embarrassment that many people feel has led to a much higher rate of STI infection. As scary as STIs can be, we can keep ourselves safer by making good, responsible decisions. Of course, the ONLY way to guarantee that you do not get an STI is not to have sex. Not having sex is called abstinence, and it is the only way to keep yourself absolutely safe. However, if you do decide to have sex, there are a number of ways to greatly decrease your risk of infection.

As young people grow into adults, hormone levels start to rise, causing many physical changes. Along with the physical development come emotional changes. These changes can include powerful sexual urges. Sometimes abstinence is not easy to practice, but it is the only completely safe option.

Of course, practicing abstinence does not mean that you have to avoid all physical intimacy. Activities such as kissing without exchanging saliva, touching or massaging in nongenital regions, and rubbing or petting while clothed are all considered very safe activities. However, if you decide to engage in such activities, it is important to set limits ahead of time. When you are in the midst of an experience, your emotions and sensations may be too strong for you to make a wise decision. That's why you need to think about these things ahead of time—and clearly define for yourself the sexual boundary lines you want to observe.

Most people will ultimately decide to engage in sexual activity at some point in their lives. This is, of course, a healthy thing, since the human race cannot hope to continue without sexual reproduction. Hopefully, however, the choice about when to have sex is made after careful consideration and discussion. Avoiding alcohol and drugs can be important in making level-headed decisions about if, when, where, and how to have sex. Unfortunately, many young people, like Kristin on her beach vacation in chapter 3, make poor choices under the influence of drugs or alcohol and end up having to deal with the consequences.

If you are going to have sex, there are definitely ways to keep yourself safer:

- Have a **MUTUALLY MONOGAMOUS** relationship with someone who is not infected. This means that you are both only engaging in sexual activity with each other.
- Openly discuss sexual history before having sex. The more you know, the safer you will be. Make sure you are having this conversation before things get too heated. Most people have better discussions with all their clothes on. In addition, do not forget that many people do not hesitate to lie about such things.
- Have testing for STIs done for you and your partner before beginning a sexual relationship.
- Always use a latex condom. Don't forget to check expiration dates!
- Know the symptoms of STIs and pay attention to your body. Seek medical attention at the first sign of a problem.
- Pay attention to your partner's body too. Don't hesitate to ask questions if you see something of concern, and don't have sex again until your partner has seen a doctor.

Sexually Transmitted Infections

- Have regular checkups for STIs even if you have not had any problems. Remember that many STIs do not have visible symptoms at all.

Male condoms are one of the most common ways of limiting the transmission of STIs. A condom is a very thin tube of material, usually latex, which is rolled over a man's penis, covering it entirely during sexual relations. They are, of course, not foolproof, but using them is certainly better than not. There are a couple things to keep in mind when using condoms. It is important to make sure that you are using condoms made from latex. Although "natural" or lambskin condoms are effective in avoiding pregnancy, they are not a good choice for preventing STIs. They have very small holes in them, too small for sperm to swim through, but big enough for some of the microbes that cause STIs. For example, the virus that causes AIDS can find its way through the holes in lambskin condoms. In addition, condoms do not last forever and are typically printed with expiration dates. The "just in case" condom in your wallet should be replaced regularly! Plus hot or cold temperatures can make them break down faster, so your wallet might not be the best place to keep them. It is also important to make sure you are using them correctly. Read the package insert for an explanation of how to put on and take off a condom.

Other things on the market today besides male condoms can help prevent STIs. A variety of creams, foams, and gels are designed to kill sperm. These **SPERMICIDES** are somewhat effective at killing some of the microbes that cause STIs. However, they are not nearly effective enough to use by themselves and should be used with either a male or female condom.

The age of equal opportunity has resulted in the female condom, which is a loose-fitting pouch of latex that is inserted inside a woman's vagina to prevent the passage of bodily fluids.

The end with the opening stays outside the vagina and is where the man puts his penis during sexual intercourse. Because this method provides a barrier to bodily fluids, it should be about as effective as a male condom if it works properly. There is, however, a risk that the female condom will break or slip inside the vagina during sex.

Some people believe that oral sex is a safe alternative to intercourse. However, as explained in the previous chapters, almost all STIs can be transmitted during oral sex. We repeat, you can get STIs from oral sex. As a result, it is very important to protect yourself when participating in this activity. Oral sex can and should be performed only on a man when he is wearing a condom. You will want to avoid condoms that are already treated with spermicides. Remember that STIs can also be passed through a woman's vaginal fluids. You can buy dental dams for this purpose, which

MYTH VERSUS FACT

MYTH: Condoms prevent the transmission of all STIs.

FACT: Using condoms does greatly reduce the risk of getting an STI. However, you are still at serious risk of getting some infections. STIs can be passed in fluids other than semen. For example, herpes blisters or syphilis chancres can be located in areas not covered by a condom. A woman's vaginal fluids can infect her partner if they leak under the condom, or if he has a cut or other opening in his skin outside the areas covered by a condom. Pubic lice do not live in those areas at all, instead preferring the coarse hair that covers the pelvic area of men and women. In addition, condoms have been known to break, fall off, or leak.

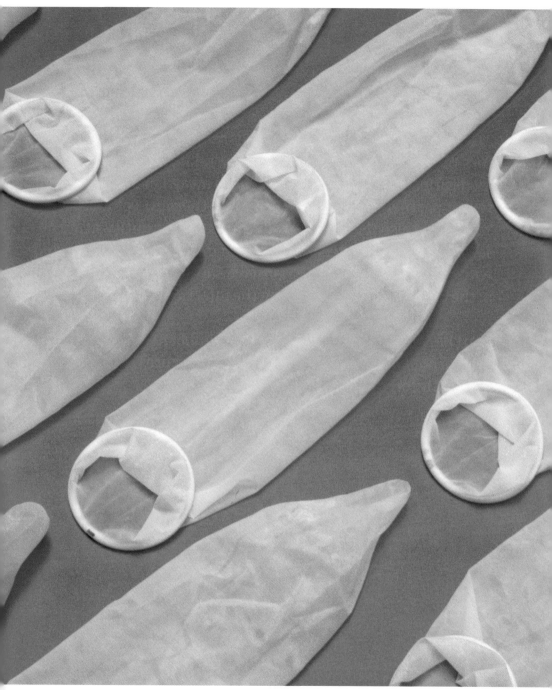

Condoms are an important tool in preventing STIs.

are small rubber sheets designed to be placed over a woman's genital region during oral sex.

If, in spite of all this good advice, you become infected with an STI, there are several steps that you should take. Obviously, you need to see a doctor as soon as possible. Think back to chapters 2 through 7 for the risks of avoiding treatment. Follow your doctor's orders completely and carefully, taking the full course of medication even if your symptoms go away. Let all your recent sexual partners know and encourage them to get a checkup. You should also refrain from all sexual activity until you are absolutely sure your infection has been cured. If you are infected with one of the incurable STIs, make sure you take precautions in the future to avoid spreading the infection.

Don't be one of the people that are too embarrassed to seek help or information. STIs are avoidable and most are treatable. Keep yourself informed and make good decisions.

MYTH VERSUS FACT

Remember our quiz from page 15? Here are the answers:

1. MYTH: Only people who have sex with many different partners get STIs.
    TRUTH: Every person who has sex can get an STI, even if it is with only one partner. Protect yourself by knowing your partner's sexual history and using proper protection when having sex. The best way to prevent an STI is abstinence.

2. MYTH: I can't get an STI because I am taking birth control pills.
    TRUTH: Birth control pills offer absolutely no protection against STIs. They are only used to prevent pregnancy.

3. MYTH: Douching after sex will protect me from an STI.
    TRUTH: Douching after sex will not prevent most STIs. The microbes that cause infections are not going to be easily washed away. Douching should not be considered a form of protection.

4. MYTH: Using two condoms is even safer than using just one.
    TRUTH: Using two condoms is actually less safe than using just one. There is an increased risk that the condom will break when using two, because there is increased friction on them as they rub together.

5. MYTH: Having anal sex protects against STIs.
    TRUTH: Having anal sex definitely does not reduce the risk of getting an STI. Most of the microbes that cause STIs will live in the anus and cause infections.

6. MYTH: Anybody that has had an STI and been successfully treated for it is immune to getting it again.
   TRUTH: Not necessarily. It is true that the immune system will learn to recognize some microbes, but there are many that it will not. Most of the microbes that cause STIs are not recognized in this way. In fact, some STIs will actually increase the risk of re-infection at a later date.

7. MYTH: If I don't have any symptoms, I can't have an STI.
   TRUTH: There are many STIs that are often symptom-free. Just because you have no symptoms does not mean you are "clean."

8. MYTH: If I always use a condom, I can't get an STI.
   TRUTH: There are many STIs that can be passed from person to person in spite of the use of a condom. Condoms will help prevent infection but are by no means foolproof.

9. MYTH: Oral sex is safe without a condom.
   TRUTH: Oral sex on an infected person is unsafe. The use of a dental dam or condom can reduce the risks but offer no guarantee of total protection.

10. MYTH: You can't get an STI the first time you have sex.
    TRUTH: STIs do not distinguish between virgins and more experienced people. Anyone can get an STI any time they have sex.

Sexually Transmitted Infections

Further Reading

Cefrey, Holly. *Syphilis and Other Sexually Transmitted Diseases*. New York: Rosen, 2002.

Endershe, Julie K. *Sexually Transmitted Diseases: How Are They Prevented?* Mankato, Minn.: LifeMatters, 2000.

Hickman Brynie, Faith. *101 Questions About Sex and Sexuality with Answers for the Curious, Cautious, and Confused*. Brookfield, Conn.: Twenty-First Century Books, 2003.

Little, Marjorie. *Sexually Transmitted Diseases*. Philadelphia, Pa.: Chelsea House Publishers, 2000.

McPhee, Andrew T. *AIDS*. New York: Watts Library, 2000.

Stanley, Deborah A. (ed.). *Sexual Health Information for Teens*. Detroit, Mich.: Omnigraphics, 2003.

Yancey, Diane. *STDs: What You Don't Know Can Hurt You*. Brookfield, Conn.: Twenty-First Century Books, 2002.

For More Information

AIDSinfo—HIV/AIDS Information
www.aidsinfo.nih.gov

American Social Health Organization: Answers to Your Questions About Teen Sexual Health and Sexually Transmitted Disease Prevention
www.iwannaknow.org

Center for Disease Control, Sexually Transmitted
Diseases: Facts & Information
www.cdc.gov/nchstp/dSTI/disease_info.htm

Health Canada: Sexual Health and Sexually Transmitted Infections
www.phac-aspc.gc.ca/STI-mts/faq_e.html

QUIZ: Are you STI Savvy?
teenadvice.about.com/library/teenquiz/6/blSTIquizmain.htm

TeensHealth
kidshealth.org/teen

Publisher's note:
The websites listed on these pages were active at the time of publication. The publisher is not responsible for websites that have changed their addresses or discontinued operation since the date of publication. The publisher will review and update the websites upon each reprint.

Glossary

ANTIBIOTIC-RESISTANT A characteristic of an infection-causing microorganism that remains unaffected by the administering of something meant to kill it, an antibiotic, which is a substance made of or a semi-synthetic substance derived from a microorganism.

ARCHAEOLOGISTS People who conduct scientific study of the remains of monuments, fossils, and artifacts (things created by humans, usually for practical purposes) to better understand past human life and activity.

CHRONIC Marked by a long time or happening often.

DISCHARGE The emission (pouring forth) of a liquid or other content.

EPIDEMIC Affecting or tending to affect a large number of people in a population, community, or region at the same time; an outbreak or product that quickly spreads, grows, or develops.

ERECTILE TISSUE The group of cells that, together with their internal contents, help form the structure of an erection in males.

EVOLVED Emitted; derived; developed, worked out.

IMMUNE SYSTEMS The bodily systems protecting the body from foreign substances, cells, and tissues by producing the immune response; includes the thymus, spleen, lymph nodes, special deposits of lymphoid tissue (as in the gastrointestinal tract and bone marrow), lymphocytes including the B cells and T cells, and antibodies.

INFECTIOUS Capable of quickly spreading a condition or illness to others; communicable.

LATENT From the French word latere, to lie hidden; capable of becoming though not now seen or active.

123

LYMPH NODES Tissues containing lymphocytes, a type of white blood cell.

MUSCLE WASTING A gradual deterioration, lessening of strength, and decrease in size of the muscles.

MUTUALLY MONOGAMOUS A couple's agreement to having no other mate.

OPPORTUNISTIC INFECTIONS Being or caused by a usually harmless microorganism that can become capable of causing disease when the host's resistance is impaired.

OVARIES The female reproductive organs essential to producing eggs and in vertebrates female sex hormones.

PARASITES Organisms living with or on other organisms and benefiting from this association, usually injuring the host.

PROSTATE A firm mass that is partly muscle and partly gland and is situated at the base of the urethra in male mammals. It secretes a fluid that is a major part of ejaculatory fluid.

SCROTUM In mammals, the external pouch containing the testes.

SPERMICIDES Preparations or substances that are used to kill sperm.

VULNERABLE Capable of being injured; open to damage or attack.

YEAST INFECTION An infection of the female genital tract characterized by inflammation and discharge.

Index

Picture Credits

Biographies

William and Miranda Hunter live in New York State. William graduated from Fredonia University with a B.S in biology and the University at Buffalo with an M.A. in biology. Miranda received a B.A. from Geneva College and a J.D. from the University at Buffalo School of Law. Both Hunters are also certified teachers and William teaches high school biology.

Mary Ann McDonnell, Ph.D., R.N., is the owner of South Shore Psychiatric Services, where she provides psychiatric services to children and adolescents. She has worked as a psychiatric nurse at Franciscan Hospital for Children and has been a clinical instructor for Northeastern University and Boston College advanced-practice nursing students. She was also the director of clinical trials in the pediatric psychopharmacology research unit at Massachusetts General Hospital. Her areas of expertise are bipolar disorder in children and adolescents, ADHD, and depression.

Dr. Sara Forman is a board certified physician in Adolescent Medicine. She has worked at Bentley Student Health Services since 1995 as a Senior Consulting Physician. Dr. Forman graduated from Barnard College and Harvard Medical School and completed her residency in Pediatrics at Children's Hospital of Philadelphia. After completing a fellowship in Adolescent Medicine at Children's Hospital Boston (CHB), she became an attending physician in that division. Dr. Forman's specialties include general adolescent health and eating disorders. She is the Director of the Outpatient Eating Disorders Program at Children's Hospital in Boston. In addition to seeing students at Bentley College, Dr. Forman sees primary care adolescent patients in the Adolescent Clinic at Children's and at The Germaine Lawrence School, a residential school for emotionally disturbed teenage girls.